AGLOW
in the
KITCHEN

AGLOW in the KITCHEN

A collection of nutritious recipes, creative homemaking hints, and inspiration

Edited by Agnes Lawless and Ann Thomas
Illustrated by Sharon Bogen

Aglow Publications, P.O. Box I, Lynnwood, WA 98036

The biblical references in this book are taken from the King James Version of the Bible, unless otherwise noted: TLB, The Living Bible; TAB, The Amplified Bible; NASB, The New American Standard Bible.

© Copyright 1976 by Women's Aglow Fellowship
Lynnwood, Washington, U.S.A.
All rights reserved
Printed in the United States of America

Second Printing 1976
Third Printing 1978
Fourth Printing 1979

ISBN No: 0-930756-21-5

Table of Contents

Soups and Beverages 9

Breads 21

Main Dishes 43

Salads and Vegetables 83

Desserts 109

Cakes, Cookies, and Snacks 129

Index 155

Acknowledgements

We wish to express our appreciation to Karis Taylor, Nancy Rawley, Sandi Gramps, Karen Axe, and Joyce Parsons for typing the recipes and giving helpful suggestions.

We give our heartfelt thanks to the hundreds of women who responded to our request for recipes, inspirational pieces, and homemaking hints.

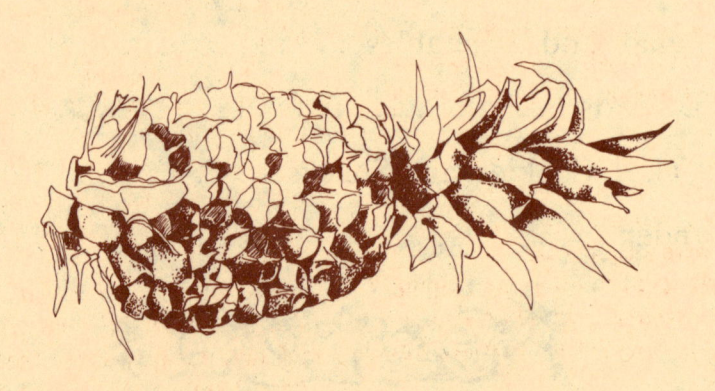

Foreword

A Christian wife's first place of service to the Lord is in her home. As she cares for her family, she is serving the Lord.

In my home, one evening, the door banged open.

"What's cooking?" my husband John asked, as usual. He lifted the lid off the pot on the back burner and sniffed. "Mmmmm, that smells good. There is nothing that makes me happier than to smell a good supper cooking when I come home from work. It makes a man feel loved and cared for."

He went to put his coat away, then came back.

"In fact," he continued emphatically, "it's downright spiritual. Do you realize that cooking and homemaking are ministries *to the Lord*?"

I was stunned. For years I had thought that there were different kinds of work: practical and spiritual. Teaching a Bible class was sacred work. Preparing meals and washing dishes were unspiritual.

I recalled that Jesus had spent many years helping His earthly father in his carpenter shop. He had done ordinary, practical, homey tasks. Yet all that He did was to the glory of God.

As I got the lettuce out of the refrigerator, and began to tear it up for salad, I talked to the Lord.

"Jesus, thank You for showing me that housework is sacred. Help me to realize while I am cooking and cleaning that I am doing them for You because You are living here and my husband is Your representative."

I remembered what the Apostle Paul wrote: "Whatsoever ye do, do it heartily, as to the Lord" (Col. 3:23-24).

After slipping into a fresh dress and combing my hair, I set the table with pink placemats and flowered china. I arranged a little bunch of roses from the garden in a low bowl, and I ladled the aromatic stew and parsley dumplings into a serving bowl. Then I called to John.

"Hey," he laughed. "Are we having company?"

"Why, yes — yes, we are. Jesus is having dinner with us tonight!"

My heart overflowed with joy when I saw how much John appreciated the extra care I had taken. I knew that truly as I ministered to my family, I was serving the Lord.

The recipes, helpful hints, and inspirational pieces in this book have been contributed by women who are learning to minister to the Lord in their homes. We hope that through it the Lord will help you do the same.

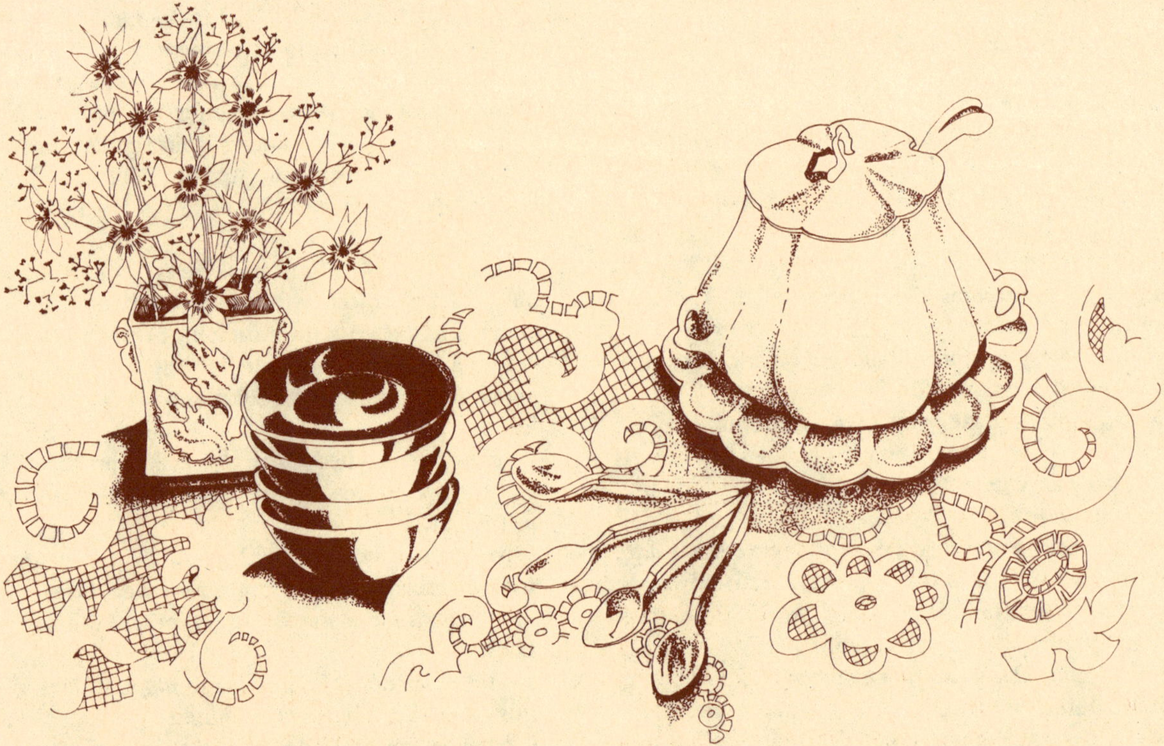

Soups and Beverages

You may have read the old folk tale about the hungry young man who talked a peasant woman into making soup from a stone. Of course, he slyly suggested the addition of other ingredients, such as juicy beef bones, carrots, and onions. When the old woman tasted it, she pronounced it fit for a king.

We won't promise that you can make soup from a stone, but we do promise that you can make delicious, nourishing, and economical soups from ingredients you may already have on hand.

Your efforts will be rewarded when your family comes home on a cold winter's day to be greeted by the smell of soup simmering on the back burner. They will realize that you have taken time to create a special gift for them to satisfy their bodily needs.

Dish your soup into a handsome tureen or serving bowl. Make tiny dumplings to float on top, or a hot bread. Along with your soup serve tossed green salad and apple pie for dessert.

Your family will declare that dinner was fit for a king!

AUTUMN CHOWDER

An excellent Sunday night supper.

Serves: 8

6 slices bacon, chopped
1 cup onion, chopped
1 cup water
2½ cups potatoes, diced
1 cup carrots, sliced
2 tsp. instant chicken bouillon
3 cups milk
2 cans (16 oz.) whole corn, drained
½ tsp. pepper
3 cups (12 oz.) cheddar cheese, shredded
3 Tbsp. flour

Fry bacon. Add onions. Brown until bacon is crisp. Stir in water, potatoes, carrots, and bouillon. Simmer until potatoes are tender (about 15-20 minutes). Stir in milk, corn, and pepper and heat until simmering. Mix cheese and flour and add to soup mixture, stirring constantly until cheese is melted.

— Sally Evert, Stillwater, Minnesota

Joy is the infallible sign
of the presence of God.

HEARTY VEGETABLE SOUP

A complete meal in itself. Mrs. Owens fills her large canning kettle with this soup, using vegetables from her garden, and freezes the soup for winter use.

4 lbs. ground beef, lean
1 qt. water
½ cup barley
Available vegetables, such as:

zucchini	onions	cabbage
okra	green peppers	collards
carrots	celery	lettuce
string beans	cauliflower	radishes
parsley	broccoli	spinach
tomatoes	chard (add last)	

Spices to taste: basil, thyme, bay leaf, garlic salt

Brown the ground beef and drain. Fill large kettle with desired vegetables, chopped. Add water, barley, meat, and spices. Bring to boil. Simmer slowly until vegetables are almost tender. Add tomatoes near the last. Pack into containers and freeze. Before serving, add additional water, salt to taste, and heat thoroughly. Note: Do not use potatoes, beets, or salt before freezing.

— Mrs. George Owens, Wheaton, Illinois

SAVORY SOUP

This is reminiscent of old fashioned, back-of-the-wood-stove soup.

1½ lbs. lean ground or cubed beef
1 qt. canned tomatoes
3-4 large potatoes, diced
4-6 carrots, diced
1 lg. onion, chopped
1 stalk celery, chopped, with leaves
1½-2 tsp. salt
dash pepper
⅛ tsp. thyme and marjoram (whole leaved)
1 bay leaf

In a large skillet, brown beef and drain. Place in slow cooker or large Dutch oven. Add tomatoes and remaining ingredients. Cover vegetables with water. Cook slowly for several hours for best flavor.

— Virginia Williams, Dodge City, Kansas

The beauty of the house is orderliness.
The blessing of the house is contentment.
The glory of the house is hospitality.
The crown of the house is godliness.

— Submitted by Claudine Towle, Longview, Washington

SOUPS

TRANSPARENT SOUP

A clear soup which Anne Marie drinks when on a partial fast.

6-7 pieces of chicken
4 cups cold water
1 carrot, sliced
1 stalk celery, diced, with leaves
green onion tops, diced
½ bay leaf
3 whole black peppercorns
salt and seasonings to taste

Combine ingredients, bring to a boil, and simmer until meat is tender; strain. Cool stock, skim off the fat, and pour into an ice cube tray. Freeze and use cubes for individual servings. Note: celery and green onion tops, and chicken backs and necks may be saved and frozen to be used for this soup. The chicken meat can be used in a casserole.

—Anne Marie McCann, Great Falls, Montana

"Always be full of joy in the Lord; I say it again, rejoice! Let everyone see that you are unselfish and considerate in all you do. Remember that the Lord is coming soon" (Phil. 4:4-5 TLB).

SCOTCH BROTH

Have a fling at putting together a Scottish meal of Scotch Broth and Scotch Oat Cakes, (see page 40), served on a plaid table cloth.

Serves: 4-6

1½ lbs. neck of lamb (or lean breast, trimmed)
4 Tbsp. barley
1 qt. cold water
1 carrot, sliced
1 turnip, diced
1 leek (not onion), sliced with tops
salt to taste
1 carrot, grated
¼ cup parsley, chopped

Simmer lamb, barley, water, carrot, turnip, leek, and salt together about 3 hours. Remove bones and return cut-up meat to soup. Add grated carrot and parsley. Simmer 30 minutes.

— Earline Horsburgh, Tacoma, Washington

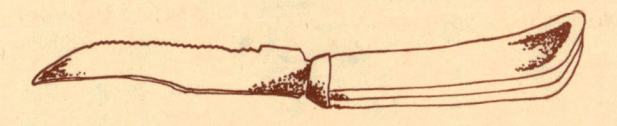

SOUPS

BEAN SOUP

Soup is a very thrifty and filling meal. Serve with rolls, salad, and fruit and cheese for dessert.

1½ cups dried white beans
4 cups cold water
3 cups hot water, meat broth, or vegetable stock
1 cup celery, chopped
2 cups tomato juice
2 tsp. salt
dash pepper
2 Tbsp. sugar
½ tsp. dry mustard
¼ tsp. chili powder

Wash beans and simmer in water for two minutes, then soak 1 hour. Add hot water and celery. Cook until beans are tender, about 1 hour. Mash some of the beans. Add remaining ingredients.

—Helen Dale, Beeton, Ontario, Canada

LETTUCE SOUP

Just before serving, crumble in the bacon and sprinkle Parmesan cheese over the soup.

6 slices bacon
1 med. onion, chopped
2 cups celery, sliced
1 can condensed beef broth
1 can cream of mushroom soup
1 can cream of chicken soup
3 cups water
1 head lettuce, chopped
1 Tbsp. aromatic bitters (optional)
1 lb. lean ground beef
1 tsp. salt
¼ tsp. pepper

Fry bacon until crisp in deep kettle or Dutch oven and remove. Add onion and celery; saute until golden. Add soups and water. Heat to boiling point. Add lettuce and stir until wilted. Add aromatic bitters, if desired. Mix ground beef, salt, and pepper, and shape into small balls. Drop into soup and simmer until meat is cooked, about 15 minutes.

—Priscilla Bennett, Pacifica, California

TOMATO SOUP

There is nothing better on a stormy night or on a rainy dark day than a hot mug of tomato soup eaten with toasted cheese sandwiches.

Serves: 6

3 Tbsp. butter or margarine
2½ Tbsp. flour
½ tsp. salt
⅛ tsp. pepper
¼ tsp. celery salt
1 qt. milk
3 cups tomatoes
1 Tbsp. onion, minced
1 Tbsp. sugar (optional)

    Melt butter in top of double boiler. Add flour, salt, pepper, and celery salt. Add milk gradually and stir until thickened. In separate pan, heat tomatoes and onion. Cook until onion is soft. Strain, then add to milk slowly while stirring.

    Note: If milk and tomatoes are both near boiling point and tomatoes are added slowly, this will not curdle. Should it curdle, beat briskly with egg beater.

—Violet Sollenberger, Lancaster Co., Pennsylvania

POTATO SOUP

Nickalene says this is good enough to serve to the president of the United States! Especially good served with blueberry muffins.

2 lg. onions, chopped
4 med. potatoes, peeled and diced
2 cups water
1 tsp. salt
1 can evaporated milk
1 can cream-style corn
2 Tbsp. corn oil or butter.

    Cook potatoes, onion, water, and salt until potatoes are tender. Mash with a potato masher in the water they were cooked in. Add evaporated milk, corn, and butter. Heat (do not boil) and serve.

—Nickalene Johnson, Poulsbo, Washington

Season your food well with
prayer during preparation.

— Letitia Heil, Festus, Missouri

SOUPS

FRESH MUSHROOM SOUP

Delightfully flavored, if you like mushrooms.

Serves: 6

1 small onion, finely chopped
1 carrot, peeled and finely chopped
6 cups chicken broth
2½ Tbsp. butter
½ lb. fresh mushrooms, coarsely chopped
1 Tbsp. parsley, chopped
1 Tbsp. flour
½ tsp. salt
½ tsp. pepper

    Place the onion, carrot, and broth in a saucepan and simmer about 1 hour. Heat the butter in a large saucepan and saute the mushrooms over low heat 6 minutes. Add the parsley, cover, and cook 5 minutes. Sprinkle on the flour and cook, stirring, 2 minutes. Add the hot broth gradually, stirring constantly. Season with salt and pepper, then simmer 10 minutes more.

—Helen Resch

"Let your speech be alway with grace, seasoned with salt, that you may know how you ought to answer every man" (Col. 4:6).

The Soul of a Child

The soul of a child is the loveliest flower
That grows in the garden of God.
Its climb is from weakness to knowledge and
    power,
To the sky from the clay and the clod.
To beauty and sweetness it grows under care;
Neglected, 'tis ragged and wild.
'Tis a plant that is tender, but wondrously rare,
The sweet, wistful soul of a child.

 Be tender, O gardener, and give it its share
Of moisture, of warmth, and of light,
And let it not lack for the painstaking care
To protect it from frost and from blight.
A glad day will come when its bloom shall unfold,
It will seem that an angel has smiled,
Reflecting a beauty and sweetness untold
In the sensitive soul of a child.

—Author unknown

CRANBERRY PUNCH

Decorate the punch bowl by floating orange slices in it.

Serves: 8

⅔ cup sugar
6" cinnamon stick, broken
2 tsp. whole allspice
1-2 tsp. whole cloves
¼ tsp. salt
1 qt. cranberry juice
1 can (2½ cups) unsweetened pineapple juice
1 bottle (1 pt. 12 oz.) ginger ale, chilled

Combine sugar, spices, salt, and juices. Cover, simmer gently 10 minutes. Strain. Chill. Just before serving, pour over ice cubes in punch bowl. Pour ginger ale slowly down side of bowl.

—Lynne Padgett, Twin Falls, Idaho

CHRISTMAS PUNCH

In spite of the name, this is delicious any time of the year.

Serves: 18

6 cups water
6 tea bags (black tea)
1 can (6 oz.) frozen orange juice
1 can (48 oz.) pineapple juice
½ cup sugar

Heat water just to boiling, remove from heat. Add tea bags, steep 20 minutes, squeeze bags out and toss away. Add juices and sugar, serve warm but do not allow to boil.

—Alsea Britton, Lewis, Kansas

"Say there! Is anyone thirsty? Come and drink — even if you have no money! Come, take your choice of wine and milk — it's all free! Why spend your money on foodstuffs that don't give you strength? Why pay for groceries that don't do you any good? Listen and I'll tell you where to get good food that fattens up the soul" (Isa. 55:1-2 TLB).

BEVERAGES

ORANGE JULIUS SHAKE
Cold and refreshing.

Yield: 3 cups

½ can (6 oz.) orange juice concentrate
½ cup skim or 2% milk
½ cup water
¼ cup sugar
½ tsp. vanilla
5 or 6 ice cubes

    Combine all ingredients except ice cubes in blender. Blend, adding ice cubes one at a time until smooth. Serve immediately.

—Audrey Jensen, Lynnwood, Washington

Lord, I crawled
across the barrenness to You
with my empty cup,
uncertain in asking
any small drop of refreshment.
If only I had known You better—
I'd have come running with a bucket!

—Wilma Goertzen, Twin Falls, Idaho

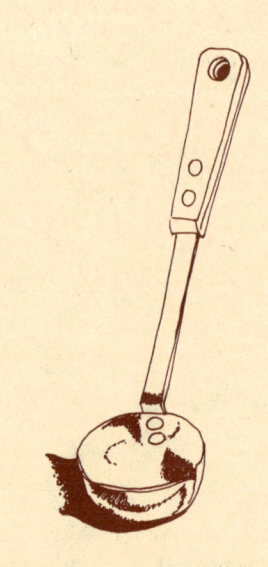

"And they, continuing daily with one accord in the temple, and breaking bread from house to house, did eat their meat with gladness and singleness of heart" (Acts 2:46).

BEVERAGES

MEXICAN HOT CHOCOLATE

The dash of spice makes this cocoa exciting.

Yield: 4 cups

4 Tbsp. instant cocoa or chocolate drink mix
4 cups milk
1 tsp. cinnamon *or* ¼ tsp. almond extract
   and 1 Tbsp. grated orange rind

Combine ingredients over heat. Mix with mixer until frothy. Serve hot.

—Debby Heishman, Chambersburg, Pennsylvania

Try drinking natural herb teas instead of coffee (stimulating), tea (dehydrating), or synthetic prepared drinks (too much sugar). Many herb teas are tasty without using any sugar. Three of our favorites are chamomile or manzanilla, raspberry leaves, and mint. Serve hot or ice cold.

Herbs are the Lord's gifts to us. They are refreshing, soothing, and often curative, as well as being delicious.

—Kathy Stanwick

Hints For Making Soup

1. The first step in making most soups is to prepare a good broth or stock. For a meat stock, use cracked soup bones with some meat on them, or left-over chicken or turkey bones, and pieces.

2. Keep a "stock pot" in your refrigerator, in which you pour water in which potatoes and other vegetables have been cooked. Cook outer leaves of cabbage and lettuce, tops of celery, beets, carrots, green onions, and the tough parts of asparagus stalks. Drain this liquid and add to your stock pot. After roasting or broiling meats, pour a small amount of water in the pan and soak or simmer it. Then add to your stock liquid.

3. Cover soup bones with liquid from your stock pot and add additional cold water, if needed. Add seasonings to taste, such as a bay leaf, cloves (whole), thyme, and marjoram. Cover tightly and simmer for 3 hours. Occasionally remove scum from top. Cool. Skim off fat and strain.

4. Cut off any meat from the bones and dice. Dice or shred vegetables. Heat the stock only long enough for ingredients to become tender. Add shredded cabbage just before serving.

BEVERAGES

Christmas All Year

Last Christmas, Charlie and I sat down and wrote out the things that our children enjoyed doing but we never seemed to take time to do with them. We had realized that parents need to spend time *sharing* activities and responsibilities with their children. We made about seventy tickets for each child and put them in separate jars. Each ticket had on it one activity that we would do with that child, or a chore that we would do for the child, or a suggested activity for the child to do alone. I typed labels for the jars, reading:

> Dearest daughter:
> In this bottle you will find
> Lots of tickets — every kind
> Of thing to do or place to go
> From swimming pool to picture show.
> Every paper marked in red
> Means Dad will do your chore instead,
> Like dump the garbage, set the table;
> These he'll do when he is able.
> Mama, too, is on the scene,
> All her offers are in green.
> She'll paint your fingernails and toesies,
> Stroll the woods and pick some posies.
> All the tickets marked in blue
> Are things for you alone to do.
> One a week you'll choose, my sweet,
> And two a week in summer's heat.
> Now listen very closely, dear,
> For maybe you alone can hear
> That every ticket makes the sound
> Of "Merry Christmas" all year 'round!
>   Love, Mama and Daddy

We have spent more time together as a family in the past two months than we did most of last year!

— Martha Woodhouse, Glen Wilton, Virginia

A Parent's Prayer

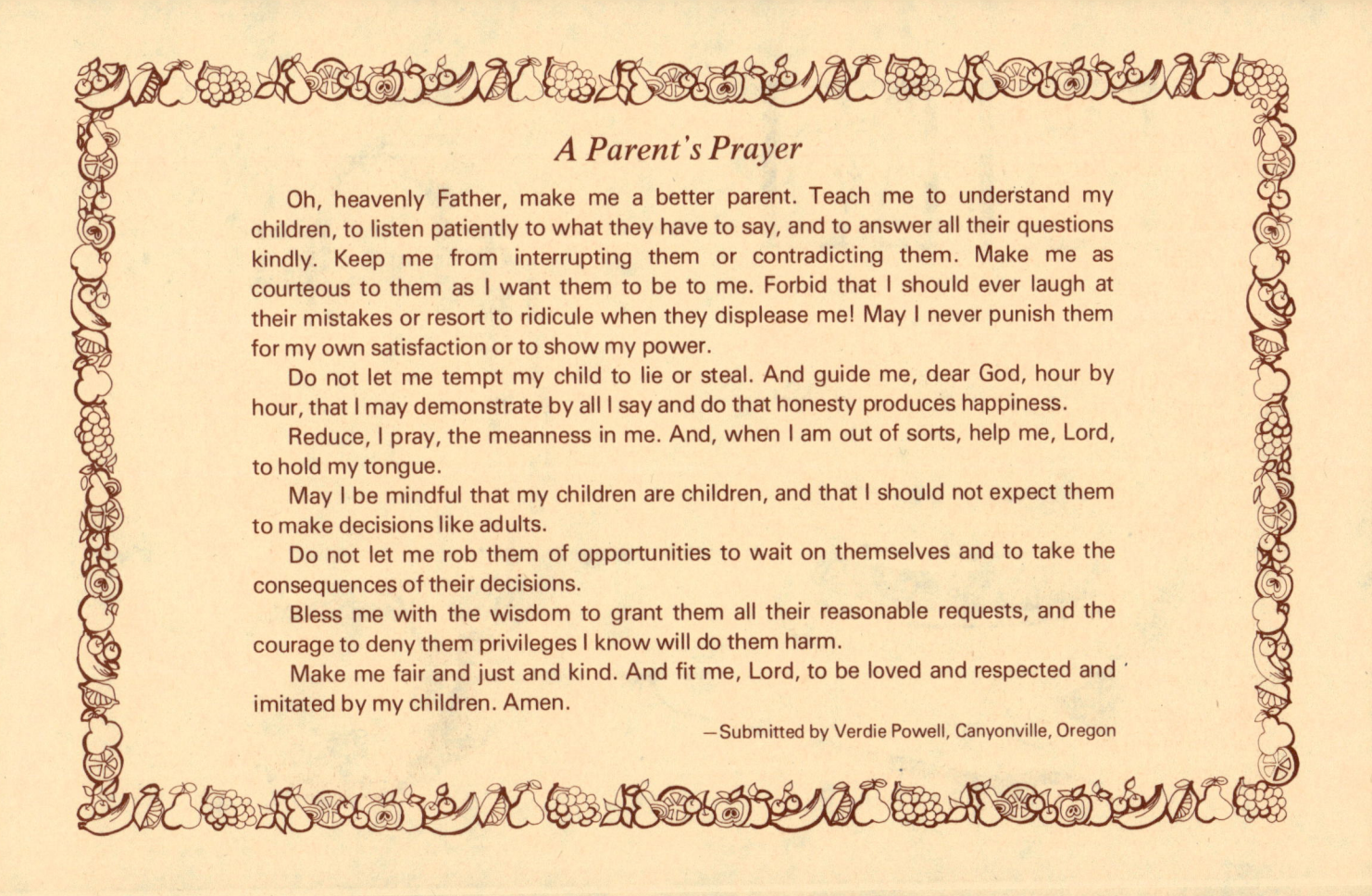

Oh, heavenly Father, make me a better parent. Teach me to understand my children, to listen patiently to what they have to say, and to answer all their questions kindly. Keep me from interrupting them or contradicting them. Make me as courteous to them as I want them to be to me. Forbid that I should ever laugh at their mistakes or resort to ridicule when they displease me! May I never punish them for my own satisfaction or to show my power.

Do not let me tempt my child to lie or steal. And guide me, dear God, hour by hour, that I may demonstrate by all I say and do that honesty produces happiness.

Reduce, I pray, the meanness in me. And, when I am out of sorts, help me, Lord, to hold my tongue.

May I be mindful that my children are children, and that I should not expect them to make decisions like adults.

Do not let me rob them of opportunities to wait on themselves and to take the consequences of their decisions.

Bless me with the wisdom to grant them all their reasonable requests, and the courage to deny them privileges I know will do them harm.

Make me fair and just and kind. And fit me, Lord, to be loved and respected and imitated by my children. Amen.

—Submitted by Verdie Powell, Canyonville, Oregon

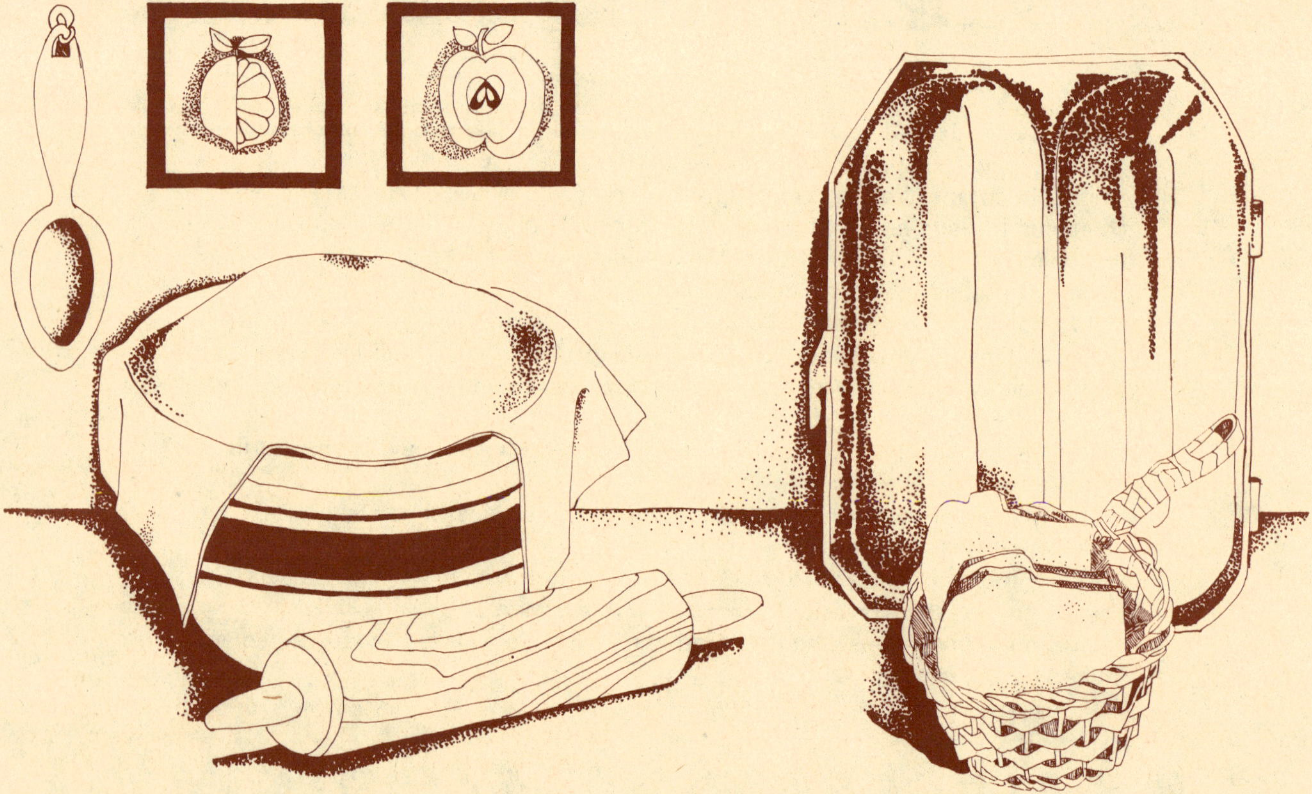

Breads

One of my fondest childhood memories is running home from school on breadmaking day. Holding mugs of hot cocoa in one hand, we children sank our teeth into warm cinnamon rolls, dripping with brown-sugar glaze and melting butter. In these hurry-hurry days of convenience foods, it seems a shame that so few women take the time or trouble to give their children such memories.

If you buy bread, take time to read the labels. You may be surprised, as my friend Nancy was, to see that what she thought was a nice dark bread was colored by caramel coloring, and did not contain whole grain flour.

Try some of these recipes, and see the eyes of your family members light up when they smell the delicious aroma of homemade bread and rolls.

We have tried to include a variety of recipes using both white and whole grain flours. If you prefer white flour, we suggest that you use the unbleached kind, which has more food value.

WHITE BREAD

Second Corinthians 9:10 tells us that God has supplied us bread to eat.

Oven: Heat to 425° Yield: 3 large loaves

2 cups very hot water
1 cup milk
1 cup cold water
2 Tbsp. honey
2 Tbsp. oil or shortening
2 pkgs. yeast
11-12 cups unbleached white flour
½ cup wheat germ
1 Tbsp. salt

Put hot water in large bowl, add honey and oil and stir well. Scald milk, add to bowl, then add cold water. Liquid should be slightly warmer than lukewarm. Sprinkle in yeast and stir to dissolve. Add 3 cups of flour and wheat germ. Stir well. Add 2 more cups flour with salt and beat. Gradually add most of the rest of the flour until dough is easy to handle. Turn out on floured board and knead until smooth (8-10 minutes).

Place dough in a warm, greased bowl, brush top with oil, and let rise in a warm place for 1 hour. Punch down and let rise again. Turn out onto floured board and flatten to eliminate air pockets. Divide in three pieces, shape, and put in greased pans. Brush with oil, cover, and let rise about 45 minutes.

Place pans in preheated oven and bake 15 minutes. Reduce heat to 350° and bake 30 minutes longer. Turn loaves onto racks to cool.

—Mary Blake, Bothell, Washington

PRIZE-WINNING WHOLE WHEAT BREAD

This recipe can be doubled or tripled if necessary.

Oven: 375°   Yield: 2 loaves

2 cups warm water
1 pkg. or 1 Tbsp. yeast
4 Tbsp. brown sugar, honey, or molasses
4 Tbsp. oil
2 tsp. salt
6 cups flour *

*Note: Different combinations of flour may be used. Soy flour and gluten flour greatly increase the protein content of the bread. For a good whole grain bread, use 4 cups whole wheat flour, ½ cup gluten flour, ½ cup soy flour, ½ cup bran flakes, ¼ cup wheat germ, and ¼ cup cracked wheat or seven-grain cereal. If you prefer a lighter bread, use half (3 cups) unbleached white flour. You can even use all white flour in this recipe!

Dissolve yeast in warm water with a small amount of the sugar. Measure flour into a large bowl. Add rest of sugar, oil, and salt. Add the yeast mixture and mix thoroughly. Knead until smooth, about 5-8 minutes. Cover with a damp cloth and let rise in a warm place until double in bulk. Punch down and let rise again. (This second rising is not necessary but helps give a finer texture to the bread.) Form into loaves and put in greased pans. Let rise about 30 minutes.

Bake for 10 minutes, then reduce oven to 350° and bake 30 minutes more. Turn out on racks to cool.

Tips for bread making: When kneading, have the dough a little sticky rather than too dry. I knead right in the mixing bowl because it enables me to have a more moist dough than is possible on a board where flour must be added to keep from sticking. If kneaded too dry, bread will be crumbly. Remember that whole wheat flour absorbs more water than white flour. You may substitute milk, potato, or other vegetable water for plain water. Be careful about letting the dough rise too much. It should be allowed to rise just until double in volume, or just to the edge of the loaf pan.

—Karis Taylor, Mountlake Terrace, Washington

"And Jesus said unto them, I am the bread of life: he that cometh to me shall never hunger; and he that believeth on me shall never thirst" (John 6:35).

Measure thy life by loss instead of gain,
Not by the wine drunk, but by the wine poured forth;
For love's strength standeth in love's sacrifice;
And whoso suffers most, hath most to give.

—Selected

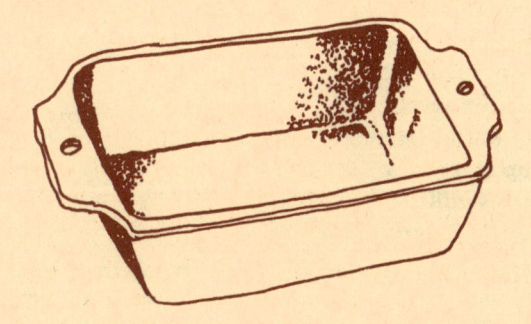

Add bay leaves to whole wheat flour to keep weevils out.

—Betty Whisman, Newcastle, California

HALF AND HALF WHEAT BREAD

Oven: 375°   Yield: 2 large loaves

4 cups whole wheat flour
½ cup nonfat dry milk powder
1 Tbsp. salt
2 pkgs. dry yeast
3 cups water
½ cup honey
2 Tbsp. oil
3½ to 4 cups white flour

In large mixer bowl, combine 3 cups of the whole wheat flour, dry milk, salt, and yeast; mix well. Heat water, honey, and oil until warm (120°). Add warm liquid to flour mixture in bowl; beat at low speed of electric mixer for ½ minute, scraping sides of bowl constantly. Beat at medium speed for 3 minutes more. By hand, stir in remaining cup whole wheat flour and enough of the white flour to make a moderately stiff dough. Turn out onto floured surface; knead about 5 minutes. Place in greased bowl, turning once to grease surface; cover and let rise in warm place until double, about 45-60 minutes. Punch down. Divide dough in half. Cover and let rest 10 minutes. Shape each half into a loaf and place in greased 9" x 5" loaf pans. Cover and let rise 30-45 minutes. Bake 30-35 minutes.

—Brenda Altermatt, Lindsay, California

BREADS

DILLY BREAD

A round loaf of bread is very homey and attractive.

Oven: 350° Yield: 1 round loaf

1 pkg. dry yeast
¼ cup warm water
1 cup creamed cottage cheese, heat to lukewarm
2 Tbsp. sugar
1 Tbsp. onion, minced (dried instant, if desired)
1 Tbsp. butter
2 tsp. dill seed
1 tsp. salt
¼ tsp. soda
1 egg, unbeaten
2¼ - 2½ cups flour

    Soften yeast in water. Combine cottage cheese, sugar, onion, butter, dill seed, salt, soda, egg, and softened yeast in mixing bowl. Add flour in three parts to form a stiff dough, beating well after each addition. Cover and let rise in warm place until light and doubled in size, 50-60 minutes. Stir down dough. Turn into well-greased 8" round casserole, 1½ to 2-qt. size. Let rise again and bake 40-50 minutes, or until brown. Brush with melted butter and sprinkle with salt.

—Patricia Fournier, Hamilton, Montana

UNFLUNKABLE RYE BREAD

This bread gets an A+ from everyone who tries it.

Oven: 350° Yield: 2 loaves

½ cup wheat germ
3 cups white flour
1 cup cornmeal
3 cups rye flour
4½ tsp. salt
3 Tbsp. sugar
3 pkg. dry yeast
1 cup warm water
⅓ cup margarine
2⅔ cups milk
¼ cup dark corn syrup

    Mix sugar, yeast, and warm water together; set aside. Heat milk, margarine, and corn syrup together until margarine is partly melted. Cool to lukewarm. Add yeast mixture. Slowly add dry ingredients which have been mixed together. You may not use all the flour — keep some for kneading. Let rise about ¾ hour. Punch down and knead 10-12 minutes. Place in 2 bread pans and let rise about 1 hour. Bake 35-40 minutes.

—Anne-Marie Quackenbush, Chester, Vermont

WHOLE WHEAT EGG BREAD

It is especially good toasted.

Oven: 350°   Yield: 1 loaf

1 pkg. or 1 Tbsp. yeast dissolved in 1 cup warm water
¾ tsp. salt
1½ Tbsp. honey or sorghum
1½ Tbsp. butter, melted
1½ Tbsp. oil
2 eggs
3 cups whole wheat flour
⅓ cup dry milk

In a large bowl, combine salt, honey, butter, and oil, stirring until salt is dissolved. Add yeast. Beat in eggs. Stir combined flour and dry milk gradually into the liquid until it is a good consistency to knead. Knead well and let rise until double. Roll out and shape into a loaf or braid. Let rise again, then bake 30-45 minutes.

Raisin bread: Pat dough into rectangular shape, sprinkle with raisins and roll up tightly. Put in loaf pan.

Christmas braid: Knead ½ cup each raisins, nuts, and other chopped dried fruit, 1 Tbsp. cinnamon, 1 tsp. anise, and 1 tsp. nutmeg into dough. Divide into three parts and braid, tucking in ends. When baked and cooled, glaze with honey and melted butter mixed, then sprinkle with thinly sliced almonds.

Pull-apart cinnamon loaf: Divide dough into 24-32 pieces. Roll each in cinnamon. Pile into well-greased loaf pan. Drizzle honey and melted butter over the pieces.

—Yvonne Baker, Colorado Springs, Colorado

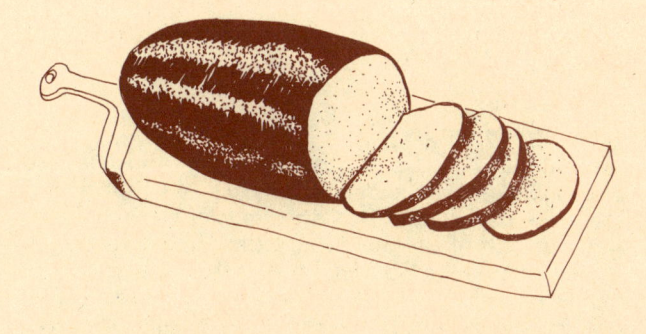

Try washing your blankets with 1 cup of ammonia in a washer full of water. They will come out soft and fluffy.

—Elaine Yaeger, Stillwater Minnesota

BREADS

EASY CRANBERRY ROLLS

The bright red filling gives these rolls a festive look.

Oven: 400°

2 cups warm water
2 pkgs. yeast
½ cup sugar
1 Tbsp. salt
2 eggs
⅓ cup oil
7 cups flour
½ tsp. mace
½ tsp. lemon extract

Combine water and yeast and set aside for 10 minutes. Then add other ingredients and beat with a spoon — do not knead. Cover and let rise one hour. Roll out half of the dough at a time into a rectangle, spread with melted butter, then with cranberry sauce (recipe below). Sprinkle with sugar and cinnamon. Roll up like jelly roll, slice, and place in baking pans. Let rise. Bake 20-25 minutes. Glaze with powdered sugar-water-vanilla glaze.

Cranberry Sauce

3 cups cranberries
2 cups sugar
½ cup water
½ orange, sliced
½ tsp. cinnamon
dash of nutmeg
½ apple, sliced
½ cup nuts, chopped

Combine cranberries, sugar, water, orange, cinnamon, and nutmeg. Boil 10 minutes then add ½ apple or more, sliced. Cook until apple is done, but not mushy. For above rolls, add nuts to 1½ cups sauce and finely chop the apple and orange slices. This sauce is excellent served hot with meats, poultry, or fish.

—Sanna Le Van, Seward, Alaska

ICE BOX ROLLS

This is an old recipe from the time when there were ice boxes instead of refrigerators. Alberta says that she has used this recipe for forty-five years.

Oven: 400°   Yield: 36 rolls

1 pkg. yeast
2 cups potato water, warm
1 egg
½ cup sugar
½ cup margarine or lard
½ tsp. salt
6 cups flour

Dissolve yeast in ¼ cup potato water. Combine rest of potato water with margarine, then beat with egg and sugar. Sift flour with salt and gradually add to mixture. Mix well. Let rise until double in bulk, then punch down. Place in large bowl, grease top of dough, and cover with a plate. Place in refrigerator.

Take dough out of refrigerator 2-4 hours before baking. One hour before baking, grease muffin pans and place 3 small balls of dough in each pan. Let rise one hour then bake for 15 minutes.

This dough will remain fresh in refrigerator at least 4 days. Just punch down dough each day and replace plate.

—Alberta Mechley, Cincinnati, Ohio

OATMEAL BREAD

A yummy no-knead bread.

Oven: Heat to 400°   Yield: 2 loaves

2 cups milk, scalded
1 cup rolled oats
2 Tbsp. margarine
2 pkgs. dry yeast
½ cup lukewarm water
½ cup molasses
2 tsp. salt
¼ cup wheat germ
4½ cups flour

In large bowl pour milk over oats and margarine. Let stand until lukewarm. Dissolve yeast in warm water. Add to cooled milk. Add molasses, salt, and wheat germ; then gradually add the flour and beat smooth. Let rise in warm place until doubled. Pour into greased 8¼" bread pans. Let rise. Bake 15 minutes at 400° then at 350° for 35 minutes.

—Margaret Knowling, Bothell, Washington

"Let us feast . . . upon the pure bread of honor and sincerity and truth" (1 Cor. 5:8 TLB).

ORANGE BOW KNOTS
Exceptionally good, and pretty.

Oven: 350°   Yield: 4 dozen

½ cup warm water
2 pkg. dry yeast
¾ cup milk, scalded and cooled
⅓ cup sugar
1½ tsp. salt
2 eggs
½ cup shortening
2 Tbsp. grated orange rind
¼ cup orange juice
5 cups flour

    Soak yeast in warm water. Add milk, sugar, and salt. Then beat in eggs, shortening, orange rind and juice, and 1 cup flour. Add remaining flour, or more, until dough leaves sides of bowl and is no longer sticky. Set aside to rise for several hours. Divide dough into three parts and roll each one out to 6" x 12". Spread with melted butter and cut ¾" wide strips, 6" long. Tie each strip in a knot. Place on a greased sheet. Let rise about 1 hour and bake for 12-15 minutes.

—Mrs. Bruce Tilderquist, Cannon Falls, Minnesota

ANGEL BISCUITS
Light as a feather — but better tasting than one.

Oven: 400°

½ cup lukewarm water
1 pkg. yeast
5 cups flour
1 tsp. baking soda
1 tsp. salt
3 Tbsp. baking powder
3 Tbsp. sugar
¾ cup shortening
2 cups buttermilk

    Dissolve yeast in water. Combine dry ingredients; cut in shortening. Add yeast and buttermilk and stir until flour is moistened. Do not overmix. Place in a covered bowl and put in refrigerator. When ready to use, take out what you need and roll out to ¾" thick. Cut into rounds. Place on greased cooky sheet and bake 12 minutes. This dough will keep well in the refrigerator for several days.

—Velma Edens, Homer, Alaska

"She looks well to the ways of her household, and does not eat the bread of idleness" (Prov. 31:27 NASB).

"Whether therefore ye eat, or drink, or whatsoever ye do, do all to the glory of God" (1 Cor. 10:31).

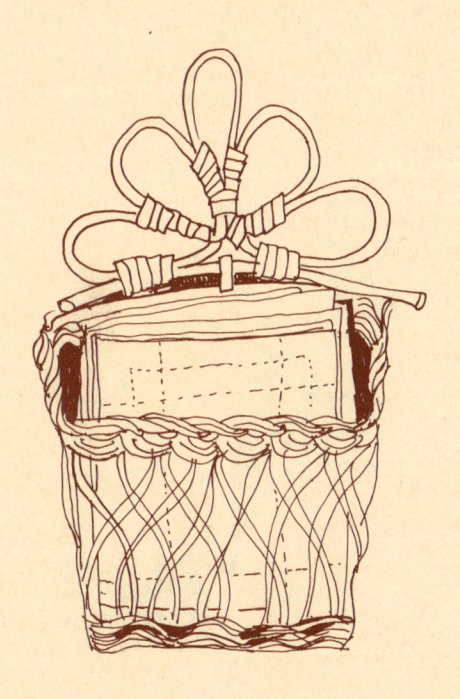

RHUBARB COFFEE CAKE

Just the thing to take to a group luncheon pot luck.

Oven: 350°

½ cup margarine
1½ cups brown sugar
2 eggs
2 cups flour
½ tsp. salt
1 tsp. baking soda
1 cup buttermilk
1½ cups rhubarb, frozen or fresh, chopped
½ cup sugar
½ cup nuts
1 tsp. cinnamon

Cream margarine and brown sugar. Add eggs, then dry ingredients alternately with buttermilk. Fold in rhubarb. Pour into 9" x 13" greased pan. Mix sugar, nuts, and cinnamon, and sprinkle on batter. Bake 45 minutes.

—Mrs. Vernon Flegler, Russell, Kansas

"The **do** of the flesh and the **dew** of the Spirit do not go together."

—L. E. Maxwell

SOUR CREAM COFFEE CAKE

A little wheat germ and soy flour used in place of an eighth cup of the flour will give an extra boost to this.

Oven: 350°

1 cup butter
1¼ cups sugar
2 eggs
1 cup sour cream
1 tsp. vanilla
2 cups flour
1 tsp. baking powder
½ tsp. baking soda
Topping:
½ cup nuts
2 Tbsp. sugar
½ tsp. cinnamon

    Cream butter and sugar. Add eggs, sour cream, and vanilla. Beat well and gradually add dry ingredients. Place half of mixture in buttered 9" tube pan, sprinkle with one-half of topping and add remaining dough. Top with remaining topping. Bake 1 hour. Sprinkle with powdered sugar when done. Cool 15-20 minutes before cutting.

—Sue Harris, Colusa, California

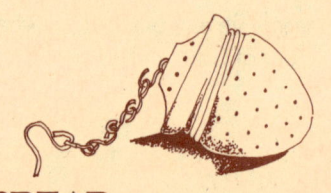

DATE BREAD

A good snack. Dates are full of natural sugar.

Oven: 375°   Yield: 1 loaf

1 cup dates, pitted and cut up
1 cup boiling water
1 tsp. soda
1 Tbsp. butter
¾ cup sugar
1 egg
1 tsp. vanilla
2 cups flour, sifted
1 tsp. baking powder
⅛ tsp. salt
½ cup walnuts, chopped

    Pour water over dates, add soda, and let stand until cool. Then mix in all the rest of the ingredients and bake about 45 minutes. Use a greased and floured loaf pan.

—Bernice Smith, Seattle, Washington

B AND B BREAD

What a terrific combination: bran and bananas!

Oven: 350°   Yield: 1 loaf

¼ cup shortening
½ cup sugar or ¼ cup honey
1 cup All-Bran
1½ cups bananas, mashed
1 egg
1 tsp. vanilla
1½ cups flour
2 tsp. baking powder
½ tsp. salt
½ tsp. soda
½ cup nuts, raisins, or dates (chopped)

Cream shortening and sugar; add egg, beat well. Add bran, bananas, and vanilla. Sift dry ingredients together and add to first mixture. Add nuts; stir until flour disappears. Bake 1 hour in greased loaf pan. Cool.

—Mary Hartigan, Hillsdale, New York

Jesus knew who He was — His divinity, His authority, and His coming glory. The Apostle John tells us that Jesus arose from the table, after eating with His disciples, took a towel, and girded Himself as a servant (John 13:3-4).

When we as homemakers recognize who we are in Christ — daughters of the King — we can tie on our aprons and serve our families. We read about Jesus washing His disciples' feet. This was a task done by the lowliest slave in the household. We can wash dirty socks joyfully and clean the bathroom for the glory of God. As we minister to our families by cheerfully cooking, sewing, and cleaning, we send husbands and children off to meet the challenges of the world, refreshed in spirit, soul, and body.

—Anna Mary Weaver, New Holland, Pennsylvania

SWEET HOME LOAF

A sweet bread, good served with fruit salad and cottage cheese or homemade soup.

Oven: 375°

2½ cups whole wheat flour
½ tsp. cinnamon
¼ tsp. salt
1 tsp. soda
1 egg, beaten
½ cup molasses
¼ cup brown sugar
¼ cup sesame, peanut, or safflower oil
1 tsp. grated lemon or orange peel
⅔ cup yogurt

    Have all ingredients at room temperature. Mix dry ingredients. Combine egg, molasses, brown sugar, oil, and peel. Add alternately with the yogurt to the dry ingredients. Pour into a buttered loaf pan (9"x5") and bake about 50 minutes.

—Chris Pichotta, Seward, Alaska

Worry is like a rocking chair. It gives you something to do, but doesn't get you anywhere.

—Submitted by Helen Hitchin, Walnut Creek, California

PEANUT BREAD

Excellent for children's lunches (and husband's, too).

Oven: 350°   Yield: 1 loaf

½ cup sugar
1 egg, beaten
1 cup milk
2 heaping tsp. baking powder
⅔ cup peanuts, chopped, or chunky peanut butter
2½ cups flour

    Cream sugar, egg, and peanuts or peanut butter; then add milk and flour alternately. Bake about 40 minutes.

—Irene Gregory, Saginaw, Michigan

ZUCCHINI BREAD

When you're wondering what to do with all that zucchini your neighbor has given you, bake this bread!

Oven: 350°   Yield: 2 loaves

1¼ cups wheat germ
3 cups flour
3 tsp. baking powder
1 tsp. salt
2 tsp. cinnamon
1 cup chopped nuts
2 eggs
1¾ cups sugar
2 tsp. vanilla
⅔ cup oil
3 cups grated zucchini (about 3 med. squash)

   Mix together wheat germ, flour, baking powder, salt, cinnamon, and nuts. Beat eggs until light colored and fluffy. Beat in sugar, vanilla, and oil. Stir in zucchini. Gradually stir in wheat germ mixture. Turn into 2 greased and floured medium loaf pans. Bake 1 hour. Cool 5 to 10 minutes before removing from pan. Cool on rack.

—Linda Nusbaum, Mechanicsburg, Pennsylvania

CARROT PINEAPPLE BREAD

Wonderful for brunch or tea time or supper.

Oven 325°

3 eggs
2 cups sugar
1½ cups oil
2 cups carrots, finely grated
1 small can crushed pineapple, with juice
1 cup nuts
3 tsp. vanilla
3 cups flour
1 tsp. salt
1 tsp. soda
2 tsp. cinnamon

   Mix eggs, oil, and sugar together until smooth. Add remaining ingredients. Bake 1 hour in 3 small loaf pans.

—Audrey Baker, Springfield, Oregon

BREADS

NEW ENGLAND BROWN BREAD

A combination of brown bread and beans makes a complete amino compound so that ample protein is provided in this meal. From an old family recipe.

1 cup molasses
1 cup sour milk
2 tsp. soda
½ cup sweet milk
1 tsp. salt
1 Tbsp. sugar
1 cup cornmeal
2 cups flour, part graham
½ cup raisins or chopped dates

Mix in the order given. Pour into a well-greased, 3-lb. shortening can or other molds, filling half full. Place in steamer. Tie waxed paper loosely over mold. Steam 3 hours. Serve hot, with baked beans.

—Peggy Page, River Falls, Wisconsin

How to Feel Good About Yourself

1. Be refreshed daily in God's Word.
2. Be happy with the way God made you.
3. Set daily goals for your homemaking.
4. Look your best, every day.

—Anna Mary Weaver, New Holland, Pennsylvania

BLUEBERRY MUFFINS

These are better than cake. Nickalene has many requests for this recipe.

Oven: 400°   Yield: 18

⅔ cup sugar
⅓ cup butter
2 eggs, well beaten
2 cups flour
2 tsp. baking powder
½ tsp. salt
⅔ cup milk
1 cup blueberries

Cream sugar and butter. Add well-beaten eggs. Sift together dry ingredients. Add alternately with milk to the creamed ingredients. Fold in blueberries. Grease muffin pans. Bake 20 minutes until lightly browned. Do not overbake.

—Nickalene Johnson, Poulsbo, Washington

We learn more from pain
Than from blessings.

—Submitted by Ivene Goemaere, Bothell, Washington

PINEAPPLE PUMPKIN BREAD

Substitute one-half cup or more whole wheat flour for the same amount of white flour. Extra nutritious!

Oven: 350°   Yield: 2 loaves

2 cups sugar
3 eggs, beaten
3 Tbsp. oil
1 cup crushed pineapple, drained
1 cup nutmeats
1 cup canned pumpkin
2 tsp. vanilla
½ tsp. ginger
1 tsp. nutmeg
1½ tsp. cinnamon
3 cups flour
2 tsp. baking powder
½ tsp. salt

Mix all ingredients and pour into two medium bread pans. Bake 1 hour. Cool. Wrap in foil until time to use.

—A friend, Lansing, Michigan

VITALITY MUFFINS

The wheat germ will give you real get-up-and-go.

Oven: 425°

1 egg, well beaten
⅓ cup brown sugar
1¼ cups milk
⅓ cup shortening, melted
1 cup flour
½ tsp. salt
4 tsp. baking powder
1 cup wheat germ

Beat together egg, sugar, milk, and shortening. Mix in flour sifted with salt and baking powder. Stir in wheat germ lightly. Fill greased muffin tins ⅔ full. Bake for 20 minutes. Dates, raisins, or blueberries (well drained) may be added for delicious variety.

—Helen Hitchen, Walnut Creek, California

FRECKLED OATSIES

Don't keep these muffins just for breakfast fare; try them for dinner once in a while.

Oven: 400°   Yield: 12

½ cup flour, sifted
2 tsp. baking powder
¼ cup bran flakes
⅓ cup honey
1 cup rolled oats
1 cup seedless raisins
2 eggs, lightly beaten
⅓ cup milk
¼ cup oil

Sift flour and baking powder. Stir in oats, bran, and raisins. Combine eggs, honey, milk, and oil. Add to dry ingredients, mixing lightly until well mixed. Fill greased muffin tins ⅔ full. Bake 20 minutes.

—Vonda Straughan, Shawnee, Oklahoma

Spray your children's tennis shoes with spray starch, after washing them. The starch will help resist soil.

—Claudine Towle, Longview, Washington

"Never be lazy in your work but serve the Lord enthusiastically. Be glad for all God is planning for you. Be patient in trouble, and prayerful always. When God's children are in need, you be the one to help them out. And get into the habit of inviting guests home for dinner or, if they need lodging, for the night" (Rom. 12:11-13 TLB).

LOW CALORIE MUFFINS

There is no sugar or shortening in these muffins.

Oven: 400°   Yield: 15

2 cups All-Bran
½ cup honey or molasses
1½ cups milk
1 egg
1 cup flour
1 tsp. soda
½ tsp. salt

Add All-Bran to honey and milk. Soak 15 minutes. Beat egg; add to mixture. Sift dry ingredients and add to mixture. Fill greased muffin pans ⅔ full and bake 20 minutes.

—Betty J. Mason, Lancaster, California

HIGH ENERGY MUFFINS

Who doesn't need a shot of energy for breakfast?

Oven: 350°   Yield: 12

½ cup whole wheat flour
½ cup soy flour
½ cup wheat germ
⅓ cup powdered milk
1 tsp. salt
1 cup milk
3 tsp. baking powder
3 Tbsp. brown sugar
⅓ cup nuts, chopped
⅓ tsp. ground mace
3 Tbsp. oil or melted bacon fat
1 egg

Mix all ingredients together at one time. Fill greased muffin tins ⅔ full. Bake 20 minutes. Drained blueberries or diced orange rind may be included for variety.

—Earline Horsburgh, Tacoma, Washington

At dinner, have each member of the family share something for which they give praise and thanks to the Lord. In this way, you eat your bread with thanksgiving.

— Letitia Heil, Festus, Missouri

SQUASH MUFFINS

Nutritious gems, especially good for breakfast or brunch.

Oven: 375°   Yield: 18

¾ cup brown sugar
¼ cup molasses
½ cup soft butter
1 egg, beaten
¼ cup nuts (optional)
1 cup cooked mashed squash or pumpkin
1 tsp. soda
¼ tsp. salt
1¾ cups flour

Cook, drain, and mash squash to the consistency of mashed potatoes. Cream sugar, molasses, and butter. Add egg and squash and blend well. Mix flour with soda and salt; beat this mixture into the squash batter. Fold in nuts. Fill well-greased muffin pans about half-full with the batter. Bake 20 minutes.

—Carol Eisele, Wichita, Kansas

"He that hath a bountiful eye shall be blessed; for he giveth of his bread to the poor" (Prov. 22:9).

OATMEAL PANCAKES

Serve with honey-butter, and rejoice in the goodness of the Lord.

Yield: 18

2 cups milk
1½ cups rolled oats
2 eggs
½ cup oil
¾ cup flour
2 Tbsp. sugar
2½ tsp. baking powder
1 tsp. salt

Pour milk over oats. Let stand 2 minutes. Beat in eggs, oil, then remaining ingredients. Mixture will be thin. Fry on hot griddle.

—Debby Heishman, Chambersburg, Pennsylvania

1. Take time to sit down and talk with your children. Listen to what they have to say.

2. Let them know if they are making you angry and suggest they stop before they must be punished.

3. When you do punish them, make sure they know why they are being punished, and that you love them and want them to learn the right way to do things.

4. Remember that they have feelings, too, and need understanding, love, and praise.

—Linda Golliffe, Springfield, Oregon

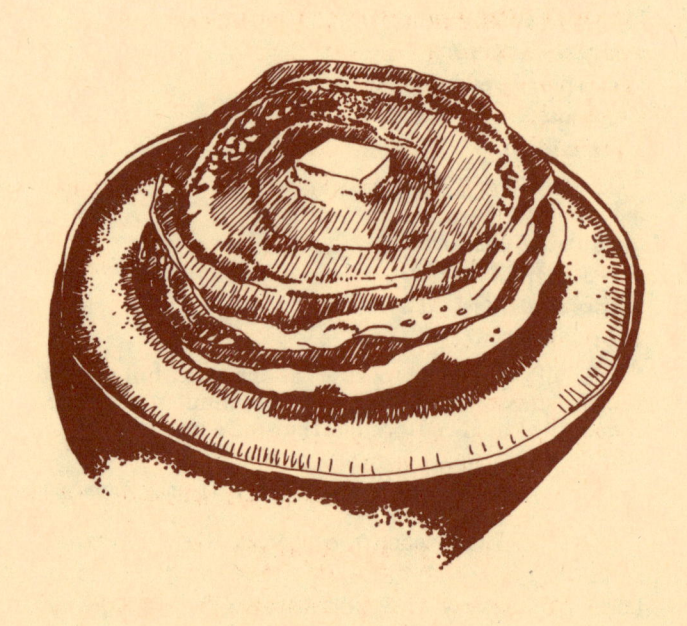

PANCAKE READY MIX

*Don't be afraid to make this large amount of mix. It makes **very** good pancakes; you won't be disappointed.*

3 cups whole-wheat flour
8½ cups unbleached white flour, unsifted
4 cups instant non-fat dry milk powder
¾ cup baking powder
¾ cup sugar
2 Tbsp. salt

Mix all ingredients together well. Store in tightly covered container.

To make pancakes: Yield: 12-15 pancakes

1½ cups mix
1 cup water
1 egg
2 Tbsp. cooking oil

Measure mix; add water, egg, and oil. Stir and use as you would any pancake batter.

—Sarajane Steadley, Springfield, Virginia

"A soft answer turneth away wrath: but grievous words stir up anger" (Prov. 15:1).

To help nourish your plants, let egg shells stand in water for awhile, then use the water to water your plants.

— Ruth Spitzer, Lansing, Michigan

VELVET HOTCAKES

These sound nearly irresistible. You may have to double the recipe!

Serves: 4

3 eggs, separated
3 Tbsp. sugar
½ cup flour
2 Tbsp. cornstarch
2 tsp. baking powder
¼ tsp. salt
½ cup milk
½ cup yogurt

Cream together egg yolks and sugar. Sift dry ingredients and combine with egg yolk mixture, milk, and yogurt. Mix well.

Beat egg whites until stiff and fold in. Bake on medium hot grill. Serve with butter and honey.

—Betty Whisman, Newcastle, California

TOP OF THE MORNING PANCAKES

This recipe uses whole grain flours and no sugar.

Serves: 4

1 or 2 eggs
1¼ cups buttermilk
2 Tbsp. butter or margarine, melted
½ cup whole wheat flour
¼ cup soy flour
¼ cup wheat germ
¼ cup cornmeal
2 tsp. baking powder
½ tsp. soda
½ tsp. salt

    Beat eggs until light; add buttermilk and mix well. Mix dry ingredients together, then add all at once to liquids. Stir until just blended well. Add melted butter last, folding it in. ½ cup frozen blueberries may be added for a special treat. You may use ¾ cup whole wheat flour if you don't have soy flour.

—Agnes Lawless, Bothell, Washington

SCOTCH OAT CAKES

Thin, crisp triangles of goodness.

Oven: 375°

1 cup flour (half whole wheat, if desired)
1 tsp. baking powder
½ tsp. salt
1 tsp. sugar
2 cups rolled oats
½ cup butter or shortening
milk or water

    Rub shortening into dry ingredients. Add sufficient milk or water (about ¼ to ⅓ cup) to make a dough which can be rolled out fairly thin.

    Divide into 4 or 5 balls and roll each out to an 8" circle. Cut each circle into 4 pie-shaped sections. Put on floured cookie sheet and bake until slightly brown, about 15 minutes. Serve warm with butter and jam.

—Earline Horsburgh, Tacoma, Washington

"I will bless the Lord at all times: his praise shall continually be in my mouth" (Ps. 34:1).

Simplicity

One of my favorite Scriptures is found in the first part of verse 6 of Psalm 116: "The Lord preserves the simple."

Anyone with mechanical knowledge will tell you that the more complicated a machine is, the more easily it will break down. My husband uses this principle as a standard when he buys any machinery we need, such as lawn mowers, cars, or kitchen aids.

I think this verse can teach us something about the relation between our life style and the Lord's work in us. The more complicated our lives are, the more likely we are to break down into tension and anxiety. The cares of our world can choke out the sustaining presence of God's living Word, Jesus.

In the area of meals and the kinds of foods we eat, the Lord may be telling us to simplify, too. I know that He wants us to eat well and to enjoy the food He has created for us, but I am sure that all of us could make the whole process of planning and cooking and eating, less elaborate.

Simplicity is a standard against which to measure every area of life, from recreation to furniture. We should ask the Lord for wisdom in sorting out our priorities.

God has said He will perserve the simple. I like to think of being simple in terms of using what I **really** need instead of what I think I need or want in order to keep up appearances. All I can say is, "Lord, show me Your way to simplicity."

— Mary Markley, Akron, Ohio

Rule of My Life

"Anything that dims my vision of Christ, or takes away my taste for Bible study, or cramps my prayer life, or makes Christian work difficult, is wrong for me, and I must, as a Christian, turn away from it. This simple rule may help you to find a safe road for your feet along life's road."

— J. Wilbur Chapman

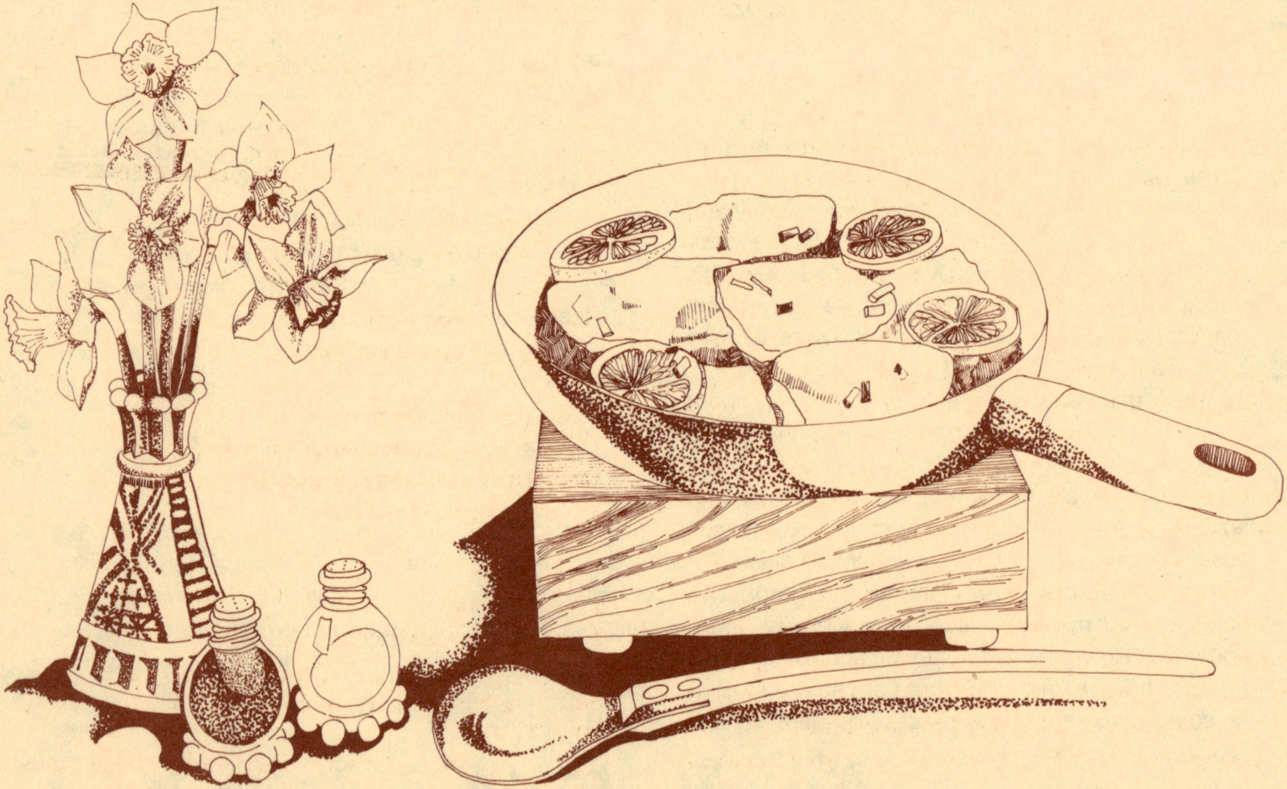

Main Dishes

God wants to be a part of every area of our lives. Ralph Martin, editor of *New Covenant Magazine,* says that when he comes home after a hard day at work and eats a good dinner, he feels the Lord ministering His love to him through the food. A Russian Orthodox theologian has said, "Food is divine love made edible." Nell Opie of Stauton, Virginia, who sent us this item adds, "I think this is a beautiful idea, for food is a symbol of the Lord's provision for all of our needs."

You can minister God's love to your family by making them a tasty, nourishing meal. If you are too busy to prepare meals without resorting to pre-packaged and prepared foods, then you are probably *too busy.* Giving your family the nutrition they need takes some time and effort, but it is well worthwhile.

Try enriching ground meat with eggs, soy flour, ground sesame or sunflower seeds, or nutritional yeast. Bind it with wheat germ, milk powder, leftover cooked cereal or grains, or whole wheat bread crumbs.

Texturized vegetable protein adds a great deal of extra food value to ground meat. Use ⅓ to ½ cup of TVP for each pound of meat. Soak, covered, for five minutes in hot water or stock before mixing with other ingredients.

FIRST PRIZE PEPPER STEAK

We called this "first prize" because that's what your family will give you when you serve them this.

Serves: 4

1½ lbs. thin beef steak
   (breakfast steaks or flank)
2 Tbsp. oil
1 pkg. dry onion soup mix
1 can (4½ oz.) mushrooms, drained
1 can (15 oz.) tomatoes, drained
1 green pepper, sliced thin
1 tsp. salt
1 tsp. pepper
1 tsp. soy sauce
1 tsp. Worcestershire sauce

Cut meat into narrow strips and brown in oil. Add all other ingredients and simmer 30 minutes. Serve over hot rice.

—Georgia Lang, Colorado Springs, Colorado

OVEN SWISS STEAK

Put it in the oven and go out with the kids. What fun to come home and have supper nearly ready!

Oven: 325°   Serves: 6

3 lbs. round steak
½ cup flour
salt, to taste
3 cans (8 oz.) tomato sauce or stewed tomatoes
½ cup celery, chopped
1 cup carrots, chopped
2 Tbsp. onion, chopped
1 tsp. Worcestershire sauce

Cut meat into six pieces. Pound flour and salt into meat. Brown in small amount of shortening. In sauce pan, combine all other ingredients. Cook, stirring constantly until mixture begins to boil. Put meat and vegetables into a baking dish, cover, and bake 3 hours.

—Joan Whitehead, Colorado Springs, Colorado

Lord, help me to speak only
Words of love and kindness today.
Tomorrow I may have to
Eat my words.

—Submitted by Skip Morris, Kirkland, Washington

BARBECUED STEAK

Serve this to someone special: your husband, for instance!

Oven: 350°   Serves: 6

2 lbs. round steak (1½" thick)
1½ tsp. salt
¼ tsp. pepper
2 Tbsp. bacon drippings
⅓ cup onion, minced
½ cup celery, minced
2 Tbsp. lemon juice
2 Tbsp. brown sugar
2 Tbsp. Worcestershire sauce
1 can tomato soup, undiluted

Rub steak with salt and pepper. Sear meat then add celery and onions and brown lightly. Place meat mixture in casserole. Combine and pour remaining ingredients over. Cover and bake for 1½ to 2 hours.

—Judy Fink, Moline, Illinois

TERIYAKI FLANK STEAK

Indoors or outdoors, this is especially good.

½ cup soy sauce
2 Tbsp. honey
2 Tbsp. vinegar
1 Tbsp. fresh ginger root, minced (optional)
2 cloves garlic, crushed
¼ cup oil

Combine above ingredients and pour over 1½ lbs. flank steak in shallow pan. Marinate 6 hours or more. Broil over charcoal or in oven, allowing 7 to 10 minutes on each side for medium rare. Slice diagonally when serving. Also makes delicious sandwiches when cold.

—Mary Ann Stephenson, Easton, Maryland

"Then I, the King, shall say to those at my right, 'Come, blessed of my Father, into the Kingdom prepared for you from the founding of the world.

" 'For I was hungry and you fed me; I was thirsty and you gave me water; I was a stranger and you invited me into your homes; naked and you clothed me; sick and in prison, and you visited me' " (Matt. 25:34-36 TLB).

CURRIED STEAK

Our friends from "down under" enjoy the brisk flavor of this meat and vegetable combination.

Serves: 4

1½ lbs. chuck steak
¼ cup raisins
1½ tsp. curry powder
1 beef bouillon cube
1 cup carrots or other vegetables

Cut up steak into small cubes, dip in flour, and brown in a little oil. Add water to cover meat, then stir in beef bouillon cube, curry powder, raisins, and vegetables. Simmer 2 to 3 hours. Serve with rice.

—Freda Banks, Canberra, Australia

MAIN DISHES

SUMPTUOUS MEATLOAF

The liquid formed during baking may be saved for soup stock. Skim off the fat after it has solidified.

Oven: 325°   Serves: 6-8

3 lbs. ground beef
1 cup rolled oats
1 Tbsp. Worcestershire sauce
dash of hickory smoke salt
salt and pepper to taste
2 eggs
1 can vegetable soup
1 small onion, chopped fine
1 stalk celery, chopped

Mix all ingredients lightly together. Bake for 1½ hours. Try it in a slow-cooker, for a change.

—Charlice Poortvliet, Lake Forest Park, Washington

"Always be joyful. Always keep on praying. No matter what happens, always be thankful, for this is God's will for you who belong to Christ Jesus" (1 Thess. 5:16-18 TLB).

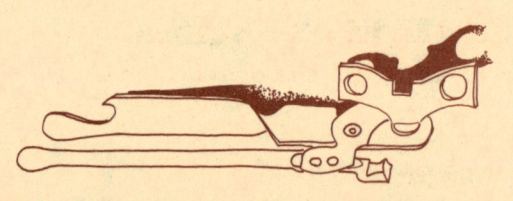

LOW CALORIE MEATLOAF

Each serving contains about 200 calories. If you complete your menu with a salad and a light dessert, and homemade bread for people who are not watching their weights, everyone will be satisfied.

Oven: 375°   Serves: 4

1 lb. ground beef
⅓ cup onion, chopped
½ cup carrots, grated
1 egg
½ tsp. oregano
½ tsp. paprika
salt and pepper to taste
1 tsp. horseradish
1 Tbsp. Worcestershire sauce

Knead meat. Combine onion, carrots, egg, and seasonings. Mix well with meat and form into loaf. Bake 1¼ hours.

—Ruby Denton, Hagerstown, Maryland

MAIN DISHES

SWEDISH MEATBALLS

There is something very appealing about tiny meat balls; especially when they taste as good as these do!

Serves: 8

1 cup soft bread crumbs
1 cup milk
⅓ cup onion, finely chopped
½ cup butter
1 lb. ground beef and ½ lb. ground pork
2 eggs
3 tsp. salt and ¼ tsp. pepper
2 Tbsp. flour
2 cups milk
½ tsp. nutmeg
1 pkg. (8 oz.) noodles, cooked and drained
2 Tbsp. toasted sesame seeds

Soak bread in milk. Saute onion in 2 Tbsp. butter. Mix together with bread, meat, eggs, 2½ tsp. salt, and pepper. Mix thoroughly. Shape into 4 dozen balls. Melt ¼ cup butter in large skillet. Brown meatballs on all sides then remove from pan. Sprinkle flour into skillet and blend into remaining juices. Add milk, the other ½ tsp. salt, and nutmeg. Cook and stir until smooth and thick. Return meatballs to gravy. Melt remaining butter and add to cooked noodles with sesame seeds.

—Elizabeth Norton, Bainbridge Island, Washington

ORIENTAL MEATBALLS

Janet's family finds this dish "very delicious."

Serves: 4-6

1 lb. ground beef
1 Tbsp. cornstarch
1 tsp. salt
½ tsp. ground coriander
¼ cup salad oil
1 clove garlic, crushed
1 onion, sliced
1 can (5 oz.) water chestnuts, sliced
1 cup carrots, and 1 cup celery, cut on bias
1 cup beef stock
2 cups bean sprouts
1 Tbsp. (heaping) cornstarch
¼ cup water and 1 Tbsp. soy sauce

Mix ground beef with cornstarch, salt, and coriander. Make meatballs, using 1 Tbsp. meat for each. Heat oil and garlic in skillet, add meatballs and brown (10 minutes). Remove garlic. Put meatballs on warm plate.

Combine onion, water chestnuts, carrots, celery, and stock in same pan. Cover and simmer 15 minutes. Add drained bean sprouts. Mix cornstarch with water and soy sauce. Add meatballs and cornstarch mixture. Stir and bring to boil.

—Janet Shellito, Bothell, Washington

PERSIAN STEW

Unusual. Don't be afraid to try it, though.

Serves: 6-8

3 lbs. beef or lamb, diced
3 onions, chopped
2 Tbsp. oil
2 cans (large) whole tomatoes
salt and pepper to taste
2 Tbsp. lemon juice
2 large or 3 small eggplants, peeled

Brown meat and onions in oil in large (4-qt.) pan. Season. Add tomatoes and lemon juice. Cook 3 hours, at least.

Forty-five minutes before serving, slice eggplant into ½" slices, and fry in oil in a skillet until soft. Place slices on top of stew and stir gently in. Cook 30 minutes more. Serve with rice.

—Barbara Peterson, Edmonds, Washington

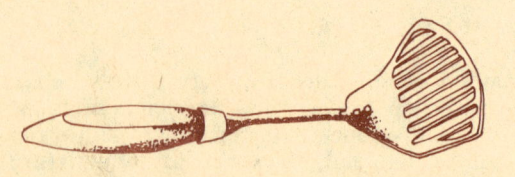

SUNDAY CASSEROLE

Named this because it is good no matter how long the sermon is!

Oven: 350°   Serves: 4-6

6-7 medium potatoes, sliced
1 lb. ground beef
1 can (10½ oz.) cream of mushroom soup
1 can (10½ oz.) vegetable beef soup
1 onion, sliced

Place potatoes in 2½-qt. baking dish. Crumble hamburger over potatoes and add soups. Add layer of onions, cover and bake for 1¼ hours.

This can be cooked much longer at lower temperature or baked in a slow-cooker for 6-8 hours.

—Mary Carlson, Moline, Illinois

KIELBASA STEW

Mary's family loves this served with a hearty bread, and fruit for dessert.

Put a kielbasa (Polish sausage) in a large pan. Add enough potatoes, carrots, and onions to feed your family. Pour water into the pan until it comes halfway to the top of the vegetables. Lay sliced cabbage over the top. Cover and simmer for 30-40 minutes.

—Mary Markley, Akron, Ohio

RUSSIAN RAGOUT

The flavors in this stew blend so well that even people who say they do not like beets or cabbage, ask for seconds.

Serves: 6-8

2 lbs. short ribs (beef)
3 qts. water
2 tsp. salt
3 whole black peppercorns
1 bay leaf
1 bunch beets, scrubbed and cut in chunks
1 stalk celery, cut up
2 carrots, cut in large pieces
1 potato, cut in large pieces
1 large onion, cut up
1 can (1 lb.) solid pack tomatoes, undrained, cut up
1 small cabbage, cored and cut in wedges
1 Tbsp. lemon juice
1 Tbsp. sugar

Simmer beef, salt, peppercorns, and bay leaf in water for 1 hour. Remove meat and set aside to cool. Add vegetables except for cabbage to water; cut meat off bones and put back in. Simmer 1 hour longer. Twenty minutes before serving, add cabbage, lemon juice, and sugar. Garnish with sour cream.

—April Dauenhauer, Rohnert Park, California

GONE ALL AFTERNOON STEW

Say good-by and leave this delectable main dish to cook by itself.

Oven: 275°   Serves: 6

2 lbs. stew meat
3 med. carrots, sliced
2 onions, chopped
3 potatoes, peeled and quartered
1 pkg. frozen peas
1 can tomato soup
½ soup can water
1 tsp. salt
dash of pepper
1 bay leaf
¼ cup sweet or sour pickle juice

Mix ingredients in large casserole, cover, and bake for 5 hours. Leftover vegetables may be added or used instead of the peas.

—Marion Shelton, Snohomish, Washington

"So don't be anxious about tomorrow. God will take care of your tomorrow too. Live one day at a time" (Matt. 6:34 TAB).

MAIN DISHES

TIP-TOP STEW

Serve with a crisp salad that includes alfalfa sprouts and sunflower seeds, and your family will have a well-balanced, healthful meal.

Oven: 375°   Serves: 4-6

1½ lbs. ground beef
1 small onion
4 med. potatoes
1 Tbsp. butter
1 can whole kernel corn, ½ liquid drained
1 can peas, ½ liquid drained

Brown ground beef with onion and place in bottom of casserole. While meat is cooking, boil potatoes in salted water, then crush (do not whip) and add butter.

On top of meat, add corn and peas. Season to taste. Spread potatoes on the tip-top. Bake in oven until potatoes are slightly browned.

—L. L. Landry, Venice, Florida

"I have strength for all things in Christ who empowers me — I am ready for anything and equal to anything through Him Who infuses inner strength into me, (that is, I am self-sufficient in Christ's sufficiency)" (Phil. 4:13 TAB).

SWEET 'n SOUR STEW

A husband-and-child-pleasing main dish. It is a hearty meal in just one pot.

Serves: 6

¼ cup flour
1 tsp. salt
dash pepper
2 lbs. stew meat
¼ cup oil
1 cup water
½ cup catsup
¼ cup brown sugar
¼ cup vinegar
1 Tbsp. Worcestershire sauce
1 tsp. salt
1 large onion, chopped
2 potatoes, peeled and cut up
3 carrots, diced

Coat meat with seasoned flour. Brown meat in oil. Combine water, catsup, sugar, vinegar, sauce, and salt. Pour over meat. Add onion, cover, and cook 45 minutes. Add carrots and potatoes, cover, and simmer until done.

—Louise Cannon, Washington, Pennsylvania

"A cheerful heart does good like medicine, but a broken spirit makes one sick" (Prov. 17:22 TLB).

PINEAPPLE PORK CHOPS

A marvelous combination of fruit and meat.

Serves: 4

4 pork chops
1 med. can beef broth
½ cup pineapple tidbits
¼ cup green pepper, chopped
¼ cup catsup
1 Tbsp. vinegar
1 Tbsp. brown sugar

Brown pork chops, either cubed or whole. Add remaining ingredients, cover and simmer for 45 minutes, stirring occasionally. Mix 2 Tbsp. water with 1 Tbsp. cornstarch. Stir into sauce until it thickens. Serve over rice.

—Beverly McFadden, Bettendorf, Iowa

BARBECUED SPARE RIBS

Succulent ribs barbecued in the oven.

Oven: 450° then 350°

2 cloves garlic, slivered, or garlic salt
2 med. onions, minced
¼ cup butter or margarine
1 can (8 oz.) tomato sauce
1 tsp. dry mustard
1 tsp. salt
2 Tbsp. brown sugar
1 Tbsp. soy or steak sauce
¼ cup vinegar
1½ tsp. chili powder
1 cup water
5 lbs. spare ribs

Brown ribs in open baking pan for 35 minutes at 450°. Saute onions and garlic lightly. Add remaining ingredients. Bring sauce to boil, pour over browned ribs, and bake 1½ hours at 350°. Baste occasionally.

—Mo Warmath, Virginia Beach, Virginia

"Get on fire for God and people will come to watch you burn."

—John Wesley

MAIN DISHES 51

FRIED RICE

This proven recipe was sent from Lutherville, Maryland by a friend of Trinh Thi Van Le, a young refugee from Viet Nam.

Serves: 4-6

3 cups rice, cooked
2 eggs
2 slices pork sausage, or other meat
1 small onion, chopped
2 tsp. butter
¼ tsp. salt
1 tsp. soy sauce
⅔ cup frozen mixed vegetables

Fry egg omelet style, turning once. Remove from pan and cut into 1" squares. Fry sausage and cut in small cubes. Wipe any fat from skillet.

Saute onion in butter and add rice. Cook on medium high heat, stirring to prevent sticking, for 6 minutes. Add salt, soy sauce, cooked egg, and sausage. Stir fry 4 minutes then add frozen vegetables. Stir for 5 minutes. Beat the other egg until frothy, pour over rice mixture, tossing all ingredients lightly for about 7 minutes.

> To handle yourself, use your head.
> To handle others, use your heart.

—Submitted by Elsie Webb, Kelso, Washington

CHINESE BEEF AND RICE

An old proverb, perhaps Chinese: "Husband is happy with full stomach and smiling wife."

Serves: 2

⅔ cup rice, uncooked
2 Tbsp. vegetable oil
1½ tsp. salt
1½ cups boiling water
1 beef bouillon cube
2 tsp. soy sauce
1 med. onion, chopped
2 stalks celery, chopped
1 green pepper, chopped
1½ cups diced cooked beef
  (or pork, or venison)

Cook rice in hot oil over medium heat until golden brown. Add salt, boiling water, bouillon cube, and soy sauce. Cover, simmer 20 minutes. Add remaining ingredients, cover tightly and simmer 10 minutes. It may be necessary to add a little more water. All water should be absorbed at end of cooking time. If not, remove cover and allow liquid to evaporate.

—Lynne Padgett, Twin Falls, Idaho

JOHNNY MARSETTI

This can be prepared a day ahead and refrigerated until time to bake it.

Oven: 250°   Serves: 24

1 lb. onions, chopped
1 bunch celery, chopped
1 lb. green peppers, chopped
2 lbs. ground beef
1 clove garlic, minced
1 can (10 oz.) tomato soup
1 can (6 oz.) tomato sauce
1 can (6 oz.) tomato paste
1 can (8 oz.) spaghetti sauce
2 pkgs. (8 oz.) wide noodles
1 can (8 oz.) mushroom stems and pieces, drained
1 can (8 oz.) stuffed olives, drained
¾ lb. cheddar cheese, grated

Saute separately, one after the other, onion, celery, and green pepper until just clear. Salt each one as it is cooking. Brown meat with garlic. Combine sauteed vegetables, meat, and all sauces. Cook noodles, and drain. Add to meat-vegetable mixture along with mushrooms and olives. Put into two 9"x13" pans and cover with grated cheese. Bake 1½ hours.

—Clara Chambers, Kerrville, Texas

CABBAGE CABOODLE

This is a good make-ahead dish. Remove from refrigerator an hour before baking.

Oven: 350°   Serves: 4-6

3 cups rice, cooked
1 lb. ground beef
3 Tbsp. butter
1 small onion, chopped
3 cups cabbage, shredded
1½ cups tomato juice or 1 can tomato soup
salt and pepper

Brown meat and set aside with cooked rice. Saute onion in butter. Add cabbage and continue cooking until wilted. Season cooked rice, browned meat, and cabbage mixture individually with salt and pepper. Put meat into well-greased baking dish; add layer of rice and layer of cabbage mixture. Pour juice or soup over cabbage. Bake for 45 minutes.

—Glora Zip, Saskatoon, Saskatchewan

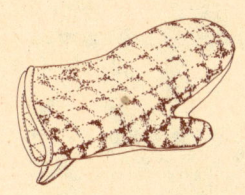

MAIN DISHES

NO DOUGH PIZZA

Kids and dads love this. Use your imagination for additions to the tomato sauce and cheese topping.

Oven: broil   Serves: 4

1 lb. ground beef
1 cup rolled oats
1 tsp. salt
¼ tsp. oregano
¼ tsp. pepper
1 pkg. (6 oz.) mozzarella cheese, cut in small triangles
⅓ cup onion, chopped
4 tsp. parsley
1 egg
1 can (8 oz.) tomato sauce

Combine beef, oats, onion, salt, oregano, pepper, egg, parsley, and ½ of tomato sauce. Press meat mixture evenly into a 12" round pizza pan or onto a cookie sheet.

Broil 5" from heating element for 7 minutes. Spread remaining sauce on meat and top with cheese triangles. Bake about 1 minute or until cheese melts.

—A friend in Washington, Pennsylvania

"My meat is to do the will of him that sent me, and to finish his work" (John 4:34).

MAIN DISHES

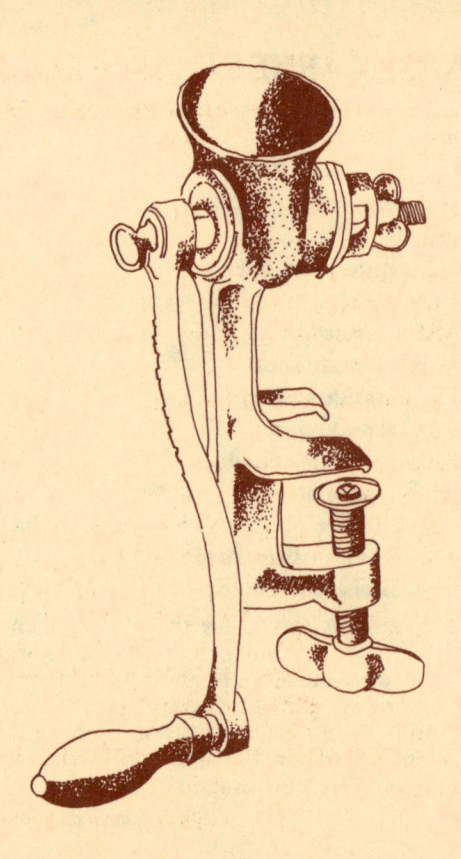

CHINESE CASHEW CASSEROLE

The crunchy top makes this dish very good.

Oven: 325°   Serves: 12

1½ lbs. ground beef
½ cup chopped onion
1 pkg. (8 oz.) noodles
½ lb. cheese, diced
½ cup stuffed olives, sliced
1 can (10½ oz.) mushroom soup
¾ cup milk
1 can (3 oz.) mushrooms with liquid
salt and pepper
1½ to 2 cups chow mein noodles
½ cup cashew nuts

Brown meat and onions. Cook noodles, drain, and place into 9"x13" baking dish. Add meat and onion with remaining ingredients and mix well. Bake 1 hour. Remove from oven and top with chow mein noodles and cashews. Bake an additional 15 minutes.

—Mrs. Conley Tilderquist, Welch, Minnesota

Add a little salt to flour, before using for thickening, to prevent lumping.

— Pauline Angotti, Willowdale, Ontario

"The eyes of all wait upon thee; and thou givest them their meat in due season" (Ps. 145:15).

TEN-IN-ONE

Don't peek or lift the lid while this is cooking!

Serves: 4-6

1 Tbsp. shortening
1 lb. ground beef
10 wieners, sliced
2 med. potatoes, sliced
1 pkg. (9 oz.) frozen green beans, french cut
1½ cups cabbage, sliced
2 small onions, sliced
2 tsp. salt
⅛ tsp. pepper
1 cup water
1 cup ketchup
6 Tbsp. sugar

Melt shortening in large pot. Starting with half of hamburger, add layer upon layer of wieners, potatoes, beans, cabbage, onions, and remaining hamburger. Mix water, ketchup, salt, and pepper and pour over top. Sprinkle sugar over all. Cover and simmer for 1 hour.

—Sara Ann Hoehn, Dodge City, Kansas

BEEF & POTATO LOAF

Men love a hearty dish such as this one.

Oven: 350°   Serves: 4

4 cups potatoes, thinly sliced
1 Tbsp. onion, chopped
1 tsp. salt
1/8 tsp. pepper
1 tsp. parsley, flakes or chopped fresh
1 lb. ground beef, lean
3/4 cup evaporated milk
1/2 cup cracker crumbs or rolled oats
1/4 cup ketchup
1/2 tsp. chili powder
1/4 cup onion, chopped
1 1/2 tsp. Worcestershire sauce

Arrange potatoes, onions, salt, pepper, and parsley in a greased 2-qt. baking dish. Combine rest of ingredients and spread evenly over potatoes. Spread more ketchup on top if desired. Bake 1 hour.

—A friend, Lansing, Michigan

"He hath given meat unto them that fear him: he will ever be mindful of his covenant" (Ps. 111:5).

HIGHLAND HOT POT

An interesting combination of beef, sausage, and vegetables.

Oven: 350°   Serves: 6

4 potatoes, sliced 1/4" thick
2 onions, sliced 1/4" thick
2 apples, sliced 1/4" thick
1 lb. round steak, cubed
2 Tbsp. flour
1/2 lb. link sausage
3 bouillon cubes
pinch of sage
2 cups tomato juice
salt and pepper to taste

Arrange half the potatoes, onions and apples in large greased baking dish. Season with salt and pepper. Mix flour with round steak and sausage and spread over first layer. Finish with another layer of vegetables and apples. Bring tomato juice, bouillon, and sage to a boil. Pour over meat and vegetables. Bake 1 hour.

—Kathy Rohde, Walla Walla, Washington

"Charm can be deceptive and beauty doesn't last, but a woman who fears and reverences God shall be greatly praised" (Prov. 31:30 TLB).

TORTILLA CASSEROLE

You had better try this the next time you need a large casserole for family, friends, or church potluck.

Oven: 350°   Serves: 8

1½ lbs. ground beef
1 med. onion, minced
1 can (1 lb.) tomatoes
1 can (10 oz.) enchilada sauce
1 can (2¼ oz.) sliced ripe olives, undrained
1 tsp. salt
¼ tsp. garlic powder
⅛ tsp. pepper
¼ cup salad oil
8 corn tortillas
1 cup cottage cheese
1 egg
½ lb. jack cheese, shredded
½ cup Cheddar cheese, shredded
tortilla chips, crushed

Brown beef in part of oil. Blend in tomatoes, enchilada sauce, olives, salt, garlic, and pepper. Bring mixture to a boil; reduce heat and simmer uncovered for 20 minutes. Meanwhile, saute tortillas in rest of oil for a few seconds on each side. Drain and cut in half. Beat cottage cheese with egg. Spread ⅓ meat, ½ jack cheese, ½ cottage cheese, ½ tortillas in greased 3-qt. casserole. Repeat layers, using ⅓ more meat sauce, all other ingredients, and top with the last ⅓ meat. Top with Cheddar cheese and tortilla chips. Bake uncovered 20 minutes.

—Doris Eaker, Edmonds, Washington

CHILI-GHETTI

The combination of spaghetti and beans gives added protein to this dish.

Oven: 350°   Serves: 4-6

1 lb. ground beef
1 large onion, chopped
1 tsp. salt
2 tsp. chili powder
2 cups red kidney beans
1½ cups spaghetti, uncooked
3 cups tomato juice
1 tsp. salt
½ tsp. pepper

Brown beef, then add onion, salt, and chili powder. Cook until onion is tender. Place in 2½-qt. baking dish. Add beans and spaghetti. Combine juice, salt, and pepper, and pour over all. Bake 1 hour.

—Margaret Riggle, Hopewell, Ohio

MAIN DISHES

CREAMY SPAGHETTI SAUCE

This is a sauce to be creative with — add or subtract according to your taste.

1 lb. ground beef
1 med. onion, chopped
1 can (10½ oz.) tomato soup
1 can (10½ oz.) cream of mushroom soup
½ tsp. salt
chili powder
ketchup
prepared mustard
garlic salt
Parmesan cheese

    Cook ground beef and onion together and drain. Add soups, salt, and flavorings to taste. Sprinkle cheese on top.

—Joanne Burlingame, Bainbridge Island, Washington

    Have a cleaning bee! Get three or four of your friends together for a thorough spring house cleaning of each of your homes. Sharing household tasks with your Christian sisters makes the task enjoyable and the time spent, a blessing.

— Virginia McGeary, Seattle, Washington

HAMBURGER STROGANOFF

A welcome variation for using hamburger.

Serves: 4-6

1 lb. ground beef
1 cup onion, chopped
1 clove garlic, minced
2 Tbsp. flour
2 tsp. salt
¼ tsp. black pepper
¼ tsp. paprika
1 can (3 oz.) mushrooms and liquid
1 can cream of chicken soup, undiluted
1 cup sour cream
1 lg. pkg. noodles, cooked

    Brown meat and onion. Add all other ingredients except sour cream and noodles. Cook uncovered 10 minutes. Before serving, add sour cream and heat 5 minutes. Serve over noodles.

—Merrily Yants, Liverpool, Texas

MAIN DISHES

NANCY'S CASSEROLE

Whoever Nancy is, she knows how to put together a superb casserole.

Oven: 350°　　Serves: 6 - 8

1 pkg. (8 oz.) noodles
2 Tbsp. butter
1 lb. ground beef
2 cans (7½ oz.) tomato sauce
1 pkg. (8 oz.) cream cheese
1 cup cottage cheese
½ cup sour cream
1 green pepper, chopped
1 onion, chopped

　Boil noodles, drain and stir in butter and set aside. Saute hamburger, add tomato sauce and remove from heat. Mix cream cheese, cottage cheese, and sour cream together, add green pepper and onion. In greased baking dish alternate layers of buttered noodles, cream cheese mixture, then buttered noodles. On top of noodles pat on ground beef-tomato sauce mixture. Bake ½ hour.

—Martha Woodhouse, Glen Wilton, Virginia

"Better is a dish of vegetables where love is, than a fattened ox and hatred with it" (Prov. 15:17 NASB).

"And when he had brought them into his house, he set meat before them, and rejoiced, believing in God with all his house" (Acts 16:34).

MAIN DISHES

The following two recipes use beef-flavored textured vegetable protein, known as TVP. To reconstitute dry TVP, mix it with an equal part of very hot water and let it stand for five minutes.

GRANNY'S PORCUPINES

Oven: 350°   Serves: 4-6

½ cup dry TVP reconstituted with ½ cup hot water
½ lb. ground beef
½ cup rice, uncooked
½ cup water
½ cup onion, chopped
1 tsp. salt
¼ tsp. pepper
½ tsp. garlic powder
1 can (8 oz.) tomato sauce
1 cup water
2 tsp. Worcestershire sauce

Combine TVP, ground beef, rice, ½ cup water, onion, salt, pepper, and garlic powder. Form into small balls. Place in ungreased baking dish and top with mixture of tomato sauce, 1 cup water, and Worcestershire sauce. Cover and bake 45 minutes. Uncover and bake 15 minutes longer. If you double the meat ball part of the recipe, you do not need to double the sauce part.

—Pat King, Kent, Washington

TEMPTING GREEN PEPPERS

An especially nice change from tomato-based casseroles.

1 lb. ground beef
1 cup dry TVP reconstituted with 1 cup hot water
salt and pepper to taste
¼ tsp. onion salt
2 green peppers
3 cups rice, cooked
sliced cheese

Brown beef and TVP. Season. Slice green peppers into a baking dish, cover with cooked rice, add meat/TVP mixture and top with sliced cheese. Bake ½ hour.

—Mary Therese Renner, Seattle, Washington

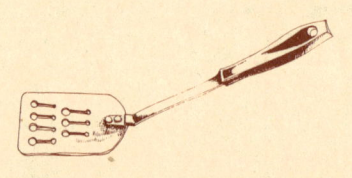

"Who then is a faithful and wise servant, whom his lord hath made ruler over his household, to give them meat in due season?" (Matt. 24:45).

Thank God for dirty dishes,
They have a tale to tell.
While others may go hungry,
We are eating well.
With home, health, and happiness,
I shouldn't want to fuss.
By the stack of evidence,
God's been very good to us.

—Submitted by Karen Axe, Kirkland, Washington

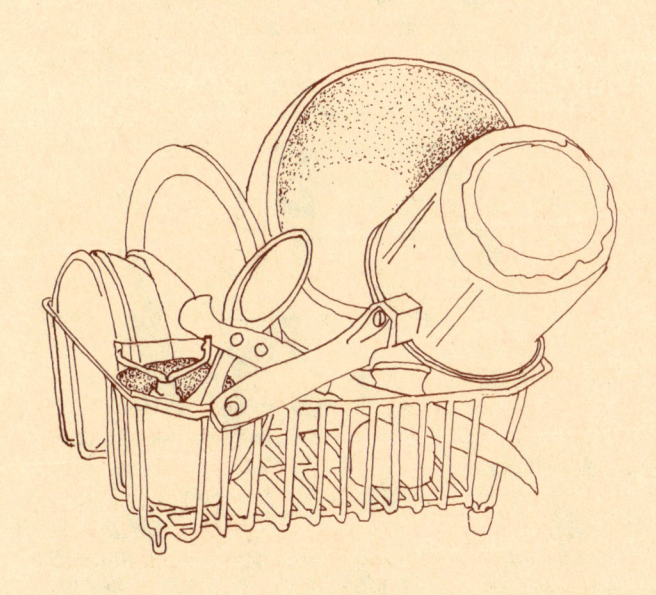

MAIN DISHES

Crockery Cooking

Your favorite recipes may be adapted for use in a slow cooker.
1. If your recipe indicates 35-45 minutes cooking time, the food will take about 4 hours at a high or about 8 hours at a low setting of the crockery cooker. If your recipe calls for 50 minutes or more (up to 3 hours) cooking time, cook the food about 5 hours on high or about 10 hours on low.
2. Browning meats is unnecessary. Excess fat should be trimmed off.
3. Reduce by one-fourth the amount of liquid in your recipe. If, for instance, one cup of liquid is called for, you would use only three-fourths of a cup in the crockery cooker.
4. Add milk products (milk, cheese, etc.) during the last hour of cooking. They tend to curdle during long periods of cooking.
5. Onions or celery do not need to be sauteed first. Put them into the cooker at the same time as everything else.
6. Cook noodles, macaroni, or rice before adding to the slow cooker.
7. Use whole, or leaf, herbs and spices. Ground herbs and spices may be added in the last hour of cooking.

CHICK-A-BIDDY CASSEROLE

One of those nearly effortless main dishes.

Oven: 325°   Serves: 4-5

1 frying chicken, cut up
1 pkg. dry onion soup mix
1 cup long-cooking rice, *uncooked*
1 can cream of chicken soup
2 soup cans boiling water

Grease large baking dish. Spread rice evenly in bottom and then shake onion soup mix over rice. Remove skin from chicken and place on top of rice. Slowly combine boiling water with the can of soup and pour over chicken and rice. Cover and bake for 1½ to 2 hours. Uncover for last ½ hour.

—JoAnn McMoran, Edmonds, Washington

CHICKEN ORIENTALE

An easy and delicious variation on good ol' fried chicken.

3 frying chickens, cut up and oven-fried
1 can (1-lb. 4-oz.) chunk pineapple
¼ cup brown sugar
2 Tbsp. cornstarch
½ tsp. salt
⅓ cup vinegar
1 Tbsp. soy sauce
1 Tbsp. sesame seeds, toasted
1 can (4-oz.) sliced mushrooms
½ med. green pepper, thinly sliced
½ med. onion, thinly sliced

Drain syrup from pineapple and measure 1 cup. Heat syrup to boiling and stir in mixture of brown sugar, cornstarch, salt, and vinegar. Stir constantly until sauce thickens. Add pineapple chunks and remaining ingredients and simmer on low heat, stirring occasionally to prevent sticking. Pour this sauce over the chicken and bake in hot oven for 5 minutes.

—Rosalind Johnson, Woodinville, Washington

NORM'S CHICKEN DELIGHT

A wonderful dish. Put it in the oven and forget it until serving time. It makes its own gravy.

Oven: 350°   Serves: 4-6

1 chicken, cut up
3 potatoes
3 onions
4 carrots
1 med. zucchini
1 can tomato soup
1 med. can string beans

Skin and wash chicken pieces. Place in a large pan and season with salt and pepper. Peel and quarter potatoes, onions, and carrots. Arrange them between the chicken parts. Cut zucchini in chunks; place on top of chicken and vegetables. Pour about ¾ of juice from can of string beans into pan. Spoon tomato soup over the chicken and vegetables then sprinkle string beans over everything. Cover and bake 1¾ hours.

Variation: Use pork chops and cream of mushroom soup instead of chicken and tomato soup.

—Cindi Nelissen, Cheyenne, Wyoming

MAIN DISHES

BAKED CHICKEN WINGS

Very thrifty and very tasty.

Oven: 350° Serves: 4-6

3 lbs. chicken wings, cut up; discard tip
1 cup flour
1 tsp. seasoned salt
1 tsp. garlic salt
1 Tbsp. Accent
4 eggs, beaten
¾ cup sugar
½ cup vinegar
¼ cup water
¼ cup pineapple juice
½ tsp. soy sauce
1 tsp. Accent
3 Tbsp. catsup

    Shake wings in flour and seasonings. Dip in egg, and brown in oil. Make sauce of remaining ingredients and pour over wings in shallow pan. Bake for 25 minutes. Turn and bake another 15 minutes.

—Juanita Cooke, Seattle, Washington

How to Preserve a Husband

Be careful in the selection; do not choose too unripe or too old. Best results are obtained if he has been reared in a healthy atmosphere. Some insist on keeping him in a pickle. Others prefer to keep him in hot water. Such treatment, however, makes the husband sour, hard, and sometimes bitter.

    Many housewives have found that even poor varieties can be rendered tender and good by a garnish of patience, the sweetening of a smile, and the flavoring of a kiss, to taste.

    Wrap him in a mantle of charity, place him over a warm, steady fire of domestic devotion, and serve with peaches and cream.

(Compiled by the Methodist ladies of Kenmare, North Dakota, about 1910)
—Submitted by Alsea Britton, Lewis, Kansas

"Delight thyself also in the Lord; and he shall give thee the desires of thine heart" (Ps. 37:4).

HEAVENLY CHICKEN

Try singing "Praise God From Whom All Blessings Flow" as a thanksgiving offering before this meal.

Oven: 350°   Serves: 8

2 pkgs. (10-oz.) frozen asparagus
2 cups chicken, cooked and sliced
2 cans cream of chicken soup
1 tsp. lemon juice
¾ cup mayonnaise
1 tsp. curry powder
½ cup sharp cheese, shredded
bread crumbs or wheat germ
butter or margarine, melted

Cook asparagus in salted boiling water until tender. Arrange in large greased baking dish. Place chicken on top. Combine soup, mayonnaise, lemon juice, and curry powder and pour over chicken. Sprinkle with cheese. Combine butter and crumbs or wheat germ, and sprinkle on top. Bake until heated through and bubbly.
Variation: Use broccoli in place of asparagus.

—Dora Smith, Hagerstown, Maryland

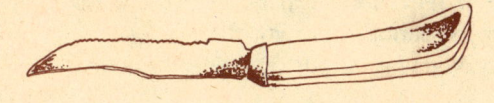

Put plastic meat trays to work. Use them under your sink to set cleaning aids on, or as little trays when giving baked goods away.

—Patricia McCash, Frankfort, Michigan

CHICKEN SOUFFLE

Have this in the oven when your family comes home so the delicious aroma will welcome them.

Oven: 325°

3 cups chicken, cooked and diced
3 cups sharp Cheddar cheese, grated
2 cups bread crumbs
4 eggs, beaten
1 can chicken noodle soup
1 can cream of chicken soup
1 can cream of mushroom soup

Combine chicken, 2 cups cheese, bread crumbs, eggs, and soups in large bowl; blend well. Pour into greased 8" x 12" baking dish. Sprinkle remaining cheese on top. Bake 1 hour.

—Betty Young, Vicksburg, Missouri

MAIN DISHES

CHICKEN-FILLED CREPES

An interesting and delicious luncheon or supper dish. Decorate your table with a French flair when you serve them.

Serves: 12

1½ cups flour
½ tsp. salt
3 eggs
1½ cups milk
¼ cup green pepper, chopped
2 Tbsp. onion, chopped
¼ cup mushrooms, chopped
2 Tbsp. butter
1½ cups cooked chicken, chopped
chicken gravy
Parmesan cheese

To make crepes: Sift together flour and salt. Beat eggs until light and fluffy. Add milk, then stir in dry ingredients until smooth. Heat skillet over medium high heat. Brush with shortening. Pour 3 Tbsp. of batter at a time into skillet. Tilt pan or push batter with back of spoon to make 6" round crepes. Brown lightly, turn and brown other side.

To make filling: Saute green pepper, onion, and mushrooms in butter until tender. Add chicken and enough chicken gravy to moisten.

Spread each crepe with a heaping tablespoon of chicken filling. Roll up and place in baking dish which has a small amount of broth in bottom. Spoon seasoned chicken gravy over crepes. Keep warm in 250° oven. These may be made in advance and heated just before serving. Sprinkle with Parmesan cheese.

—Laurilie Carpenter, Edmonds, Washington

The Tongue

"The boneless tongue, so small and weak
Can crush and kill," declared the Greek.
The Persian proverb wisely saith:
"A lengthy tongue, an early death."
Sometimes it takes this form instead:
"Don't let your tongue cut off your head."
"The tongue can speak a word whose speed,"
The Chinese say, "outstrips the steed."
While Arab sages this impart:
"The tongue's great storehouse is the heart."
From Hebrew wit the maxim's sprung:
"Though feet should slip, don't let the tongue."
A verse in Scripture crowns the whole:
"Who keeps his tongue doth keep his soul."

—Author unknown

CHICKEN ENCHILADAS

Put this together on Saturday and on Sunday, take it out of the refrigerator before church. Pop it in the oven when you get home and let it bake while you set the table and make a salad.

Oven: 350°   Serves: 6

3 lbs. chicken, cooked and boned
1 cup chicken broth
1 can cream of chicken soup
1 can cream of mushroom soup
1 tsp. chili powder
4 tsp. minced onion
⅛ tsp. garlic powder
¼ tsp. black pepper
¼ tsp. Tabasco sauce
4 cups Doritos chips
8 oz. sharp cheese, grated

Combine and heat soups with seasonings, onion, and broth, mixing well. Cover bottom of 9" x 13" baking dish with chips, then layer chicken, half the sauce, and cheese on top. Repeat, ending with cheese. Bake 25-30 minutes. May be made ahead and refrigerated or frozen.

—Merrily Yants, Liverpool, Texas

JAPANESE CHICKEN

Has a piquant oriental flavor the whole family will love.

Oven: Heat to 400°   Serves: 4-6

1 fryer chicken, cut up
1 cup soy sauce
¼ cup sugar
¼ tsp. ginger or ginger root, chopped
1 garlic clove
1 tsp. honey

Put chicken in baking pan, skin side up. Heat and pour other ingredients on top of chicken. Bake 10 minutes at 400° then 45 minutes at 350°, basting with liquid every 15 minutes. Drain and serve.

—Ann Dahl, Bothell, Washington

MAIN DISHES

TURKEY ROYALE

Take this with you to a potluck, and people will gobble it up. Praise the Lord for the variety of foods He gives us!

Oven: 350°   Serves: 8-12

1 box (12-14 oz.) seasoned dressing (bread stuffing)
½ cup butter, melted
1 cup warm water
2½ cups or more cooked turkey (or chicken)
½ cup onion, finely chopped
½ cup celery, finely chopped
¼ cup green onion tops or chives, finely chopped
¾ cup mayonnaise
¾ tsp. salt
2 eggs
1½ cups milk
1 can cream of mushroom soup
mild or sharp cheese, grated

Combine dressing, butter, and water. Toss until dressing is moist. Place ½ of it in a greased 9"x13" pan.

Remove skin from turkey and dice. Combine with onion, celery, chives, mayonnaise, and salt. Mix thoroughly. Spread gently over the layer of dressing, then scatter remaining dressing on top.

Beat eggs and milk together. Pour evenly over layered casserole. Cover and refrigerate overnight.

Remove casserole from refrigerator 1 hour before serving. Spread soup on top and bake 40 minutes uncovered. Spread with grated cheese and bake 10 minutes more.

— Naomi Homme, Anchorage, Alaska

HENNY-PENNY HOT POT

This hot "salad" will be one of your favorites.

Oven: 350°   Serves: 4-6

¾ cup mayonnaise
1 tsp. salt
1 Tbsp. lemon juice
1 cup celery, chopped
1 cup mushrooms, sliced
¼ cup toasted almonds
¼ cup onion, chopped
½ cup cheddar cheese, grated
2 cups chicken, cooked, cubed
1 cup potato chips, crushed

Mix mayonnaise, salt, lemon juice together in 2-qt. baking dish. Stir in celery, mushrooms, almonds, onion, and grated cheese. Fold in chicken and bake 15 minutes. Remove from oven and sprinkle potato chips on top and bake 10 minutes more.

— Mrs. Conley Tilderquist, Welch, Minnesota

Time-saving recipes are a blessing only if we use the saved time in a blessed way.

—Letitia Heil, Festus, Missouri

TUNA LOAF

A really delicious loaf. If you have big eaters in your family, you had better double the recipe!

Oven: 350°   Serves: 3-4

1 can (6½ oz.) tuna
¼ cup quick rolled oats
2 eggs, beaten
½ cup cottage cheese
2 or 3 tsp. dry onion soup mix
¼ tsp. pepper
½ tsp. prepared mustard
1 Tbsp. mayonnaise
3 Tbsp. dry bread crumbs
1 tsp. butter, melted

Mix all together, except last two ingredients, and put into small loaf pan. Sprinkle with topping of bread crumbs and butter, then sprinkle with a little paprika. Bake 35 minutes.

— Mrs. Richard Marquette, Lincoln, Nebraska

SALMON LOAF

A can of salmon on the shelf and this recipe and you are always ready for whoever drops in.

Oven: 350°   Serves: 4-6

1 cup bread crumbs
1 cup milk, scalded
1 can (1 lb.) salmon
1 tsp. salt
1½ Tbsp. butter
1 Tbsp. onion, minced
2 egg yolks, beaten
1 tsp. lemon juice
2 tsp. parsley, minced
2 egg whites, stiffly beaten

Soak bread crumbs in scalded milk. Add rest of ingredients, folding in beaten egg whites last. Place in well-greased baking dish. Bake 35-45 minutes.

— Ruth Lohrer, Seattle, Washington

To clean your stove racks, broiler pans, and burner bibs, soak in a solution of coffee pot cleaner and water. Soak for a few hours in the bath tub, so they can lay flat and be covered with the solution.

—Evelyn Daniel, Sonora, California

MAIN DISHES

DEEP SEA MEDLEY

It won't take long before this is an "old favorite".

Oven: 300°   Serves: 10

1 cup celery, diced
¼ cup onion, chopped
1 green pepper, chopped
½ cup margerine
2 Tbsp. margerine
3 Tbsp. flour
1 tsp. Worcestershire sauce
dash of cayenne
1½ cups milk
1 can each crab, shrimp, and tuna
1 can mushrooms
1 cup mayonnaise
1 cup rice cooked in 3 cups water
1½ cups soda cracker crumbs

Saute celery, onion, and pepper in ½ cup margerine for 20 minutes. In another pan, melt 2 Tbsp. margerine over low heat, then blend in flour and seasonings. Stirring constantly, pour in milk and boil for 1 minute.

Mix seafood, mushrooms, and mayonnaise. Combine with celery mixture and sauce. Place over rice and sprinkle cracker crumbs over. Bake 30-40 minutes in a shallow pan or 1½ hours in a deep pan.

— Ruth Tervol, Milton, Washington

SUPER FISH AND CHEESE

What fun! A seafood casserole that blends its flavors while you sleep or work.

Oven: 350°   Serves: 4-6

1 can (7½ oz.) crab, tuna, salmon, or shrimp
1 cup uncooked shell macaroni
1 cup cheddar cheese, shredded
1 can cream of mushroom soup
1 soup can milk
2 hard-boiled eggs, cut up
1 Tbsp. chives, chopped

Combine all ingredients in deep 1-qt. casserole. Cover and refrigerate at least 8 hours. Bake, covered, for 1 hour. Sprinkle with paprika.

— Marion Shelton, Snohomish, Washington

PIGGYBANK TUNA BAKE

This casserole stores well in the refrigerator and is easily reheated, if you need to make it in advance.

Oven: 350°   Serves: 4-6

1 can tuna
1 cup peas
1 cup milk and liquid from peas
4 hard-boiled eggs, sliced
1 can cream of mushroom soup
soda crackers

Cover bottom of baking dish with 20-25 crumbled crackers. Over this put a layer each of tuna, eggs, and peas. Top with more crumbled crackers. Mix milk, liquid from peas, and mushroom soup. Pour over. Bake 1 hour, or until golden brown.

— Etta Schafer, Topeka, Kansas

GOOD 'n QUICK CASSEROLE

This is very good (and thrifty, too) when a crowd drops in for dinner.

Oven: 350°   Serves: 8

2 cups noodles, cooked until just tender
1 can cream of mushroom soup
1 cup milk
¼ lb. pimento cheese, diced
2 hard-boiled eggs, chopped
1 can (7 oz.) tuna
6 Tbsp. flaked cereal crumbs
melted butter

Empty soup into a saucepan and stir well. Add milk and heat, then cheese, stirring until it melts. Combine noodles, eggs, tuna, and sauce. Put into buttered casserole, and sprinkle with crumbs. Drizzle melted butter over the top. Bake 25-30 minutes.

— Diane Taylor, Springfield, Oregon

"If you can find a truly good wife, she is worth more than precious gems! Her husband can trust her, and she will richly satisfy his needs. She will not hinder him, but help him all her life" (Prov. 31:10-12 TLB).

The Shaping of a Disciple

When God wants to drill a man and thrill a man
and skill a man,
When God wants to mold a man to play for Him
the noblest part,
When He yearns with all His heart to build so great
and bold a man
That all the world shall be amazed;
Then watch God's methods, watch His ways,
How He ruthlessly perfects whom He royally elects.
How He hammers him and hurts him, and with mighty
blows transforms him,
Making shapes and forms which only God Himself
can understand.
Even while His man is crying, lifting up beseeching
hands,
Yet God bends, but never breaks when man's good
He undertakes,
When He uses whom He chooses, and with every
purpose fuses,
Man to act and act to man, as it was when He began,
When God tries His splendor out,
Man will know what He is about.

— Submitted by Ivene Goemaere, Bothell, Washington

SHRIMP AND CRAB COMBO

Jazz up your menu with this dish the next time you want to treat your family like royalty.

Oven: 325°   Serves: 6-8

8 slices bread
1 can shrimp
1 can crab
1 cup celery, diced
1 small onion, minced
½ cup mayonnaise
4 eggs, beaten
1 cup milk
1 can cream of mushroom soup
grated cheese

Remove crusts from bread and dice. Put half of bread in a 9"x12" buttered pan. Mix shrimp, crab, celery, onion, and mayonnaise. Spread over bread in pan. Top with rest of bread cubes. Beat eggs and milk together and pour over mixture. Refrigerate overnight. Before baking cover with cream of mushroom soup and top with cheese. Bake 1 hour.

— Bernice Smith, Seattle, Washington

DEEP DISH CRAB PIE

A yummy casserole using canned crab.

Oven: 425°   Serves: 6-8

1 med. onion, chopped
1 green pepper, seeded and chopped
4 Tbsp. butter
3 Tbsp. flour
1 tsp. dry mustard
1 cup milk
2 cups (½ lb.) sharp Cheddar cheese, grated
1 can (large) tomatoes, drained and chopped
1 tsp. salt
¼ tsp. pepper
1 Tbsp. Worcestershire sauce
1 can (7½ oz.) flaked crab
2 cups biscuit mix
⅔ cup milk

Saute onion and green pepper in butter until soft. Blend flour and mustard and stir in. Stirring constantly, pour in 1 cup milk and cook until thickened. Add 1 cup of the grated cheese. Stir until melted. Mix in tomatoes, salt, pepper, Worcestershire sauce, and crab. Turn into a 2½-qt. casserole.

Cut the other cup of grated cheese into the biscuit mix. Stir in ⅔ cup milk. Drop dough in mounds on the hot crab mixture. Bake covered for 30 minutes. Remove lid to brown the tops of the biscuits.

— Peggy Page, River Falls, Wisconsin

Take time to read the Bible: it is the foundation of knowledge.
Take time to worship: it is the highway of reverence and washes the dust of earth from our eyes.
Take time to love: it is a sacrament of life given to God.
Take time to praise and give thanks: it is good to honor our Father from whom all good things come.
Take time to pray: it makes a closer walk with Him.

— Submitted by Belva Miller, Cairo, Illinois

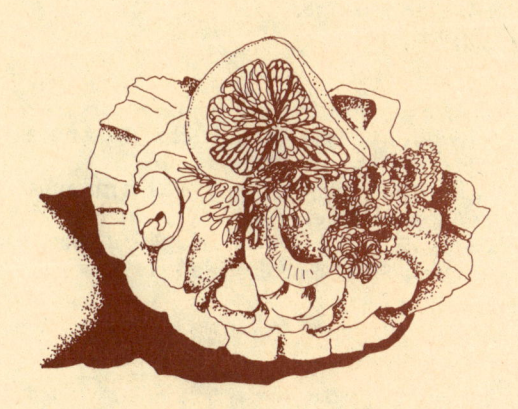

MAIN DISHES

ALASKAN CRAB SUPREME

Combined with a green vegetable, salad, and hot rolls, this makes a "special" meal. It's also a real timesaver.

Oven: 450°   Serves: 6

1½ cups soft bread crumbs
1½ cups canned milk
2 cups fresh crab meat or
   1 can (13 oz.) crab meat
5 hard-cooked eggs
½ tsp. dry mustard
⅛ tsp. red cayenne pepper
1½ tsp. salt
½ cup butter, melted

Cut fresh crab into 1½ inch squares. Separate the yolks and whites of eggs. Thinly slice the whites and mix with bread crumbs, milk, and crab.

Mash the egg yolks and mix well with mustard, pepper, salt, and butter. Combine with first mixture and mix well. Pour into well-greased 9"x 9" pan. Bake 15-20 minutes. If prepared ahead, refrigerate until baked.

— Naomi Homme, Anchorage, Alaska

"It is better to live in the corner of an attic than with a crabby woman in a lovely home" (Prov. 21:9 TLB).

SANDWICH SOUFFLE

Perfect for a luncheon!

Oven: 350°   Serves: 6-8

6 eggs
2 cups milk
2 tsp. dry mustard
bread, crusts cut off
sliced ham
sharp cheddar cheese, grated
1 cup potato chips, crushed
¼ cup butter

Beat eggs, milk, and mustard until foamy. Grease 9"x13" pan. Line pan with layers of bread, ham, cheese, ending with layer of bread. Pour egg mixture over bread. Refrigerate overnight. Before baking sprinkle potato chips on top, dab on butter. Bake 1 hour.

— Darlene Willis, Hazelwood, Missouri

Words

The six most important words in the English language: I admit I made a mistake.

The five most important words: You did a good job.

The four most important words: What is your opinion?

The three most important words: If you please.

The two most important words: Thank you.

The one most important word: We.

The least important word: I

— Anonymous

Give your children something interesting to look at while they are at the dining table. Do they see a blank wall? Try a scenic or religious picture for small children. Wallpaper with a farm scene can stimulate their thinking and discussion. Scripture wall mottos will influence the entire family for good.

— Helen Hitchin, Walnut Creek, California

EGGS BENEDICT

This was Cheri's husband's favorite breakfast when he was working swing shift.

4 English muffins, split
4 eggs, poached
4 slices ham, fried
2 Tbsp. butter
2 Tbsp. flour
dash salt
1½ cups milk
¼ cup cheese, diced
1 egg yolk

Melt butter in top of double boiler. Stir in flour and salt. Add milk slowly, stirring constantly. Add cheese, stirring until melted. Stir in egg yolk.

Toast muffins. Place ham on muffin halves. Top with poached egg. Pour cheese sauce over and sprinkle with paprika.

— Cheri Metteer, Kirkland, Washington

MAIN DISHES

SOY BEAN BAKE

Your family will never guess that this dish is made from soy beans! Very nutritious.

Oven: 300°   Serves 6-8

1½ cups soy beans
4 cups water
⅛ lb. salt pork, diced or diced raw bacon
¾ cup onion, diced
⅛ cup dark molasses
1 Tbsp. dry mustard
1 Tbsp. prepared mustard
1 Tbsp. Worcestershire sauce
1½ tsp. salt
⅛ cup brown sugar
1 can (8-oz.) tomato sauce

Cover soy beans with water and soak overnight. Without draining beans, place in large baking dish, with cover. Add remaining ingredients except tomato sauce and mix well. Bake, covered, for 4 hours, or until beans are almost tender. Remove from oven and stir in tomato sauce. Bake, uncovered for two more hours, or until beans are tender.

—Agnes Lawless, Bothell, Washington

VERMONT BEANS

Wonderful for a potluck meal or a picnic.

Oven: 300°   Serves: 20

3 lg. onions
1 cup brown sugar
1 tsp. salt
1 tsp. dry mustard
½ cup vinegar
8 slices of bacon, cooked
2 cans butter beans, drained
1 can green lima beans, drained
1 can (lg.) baked beans

Slice or chop onions. Put in skillet with butter and lima beans. Add sugar, salt, mustard, vinegar. Simmer 20 minutes covered. Combine with the baked beans in a 3-qt. casserole. Sprinkle crumbled bacon on top and cover. Cook for 2 hours, uncovering the last hour.

—Anne-Marie Quackenbush, Chester, Vermont

"Fix your thoughts on what is true and good and right. Think about things that are pure and lovely, and dwell on the fine, good things in others. Think about all you can praise God for and be glad about" (Phil. 4:8 TLB).

CALICO BEANS

Any combination of kinds of beans can be used.

Oven: 350° Serves: 6-8

1 lb. ground beef
¼ lb. bacon, chopped
1 cup onion, chopped
1 cup green pepper, chopped
1 Tbsp. vinegar
1 Tbsp. prepared mustard
½ cup ketchup
¾ cup brown sugar
1 can each limas, kidney, baked beans, drained

Fry bacon, beef, onion, and green pepper until meat is done. Combine with remaining ingredients in a large baking dish. Bake for 1½ hours.

—Ramona Pinkerton, Olympia, Washington

LENTIL LOAF

A good meat substitute.

Oven: 375° Serves: 8

2 cups lentils, cooked
1 med. onion, minced
1 cup walnuts, ground (optional)
2 eggs, beaten*
1 can (14 oz.) evaporated milk*
¼ cup salad oil
2 cups bread crumbs
¼ tsp. thyme
½ tsp. salt
½ tsp. monosodium glutamate (optional)

Brown minced onion in part of oil. Add cooked lentils and all other ingredients. Mix well. Bake in well-oiled loaf pan for 1 hour. Serve with any desired gravy or with cranberry sauce.

* 1 cup tomato juice or soy milk may be substituted if eggs and milk are omitted.

—Dorothy Knotts, Saratoga, California

MAIN DISHES

PICNIC BURGOO
Quick and different.

Serves: 8-10

1½ lbs. ground beef
2 Tbsp. vinegar
½ cup water
1 cup ketchup
2 tsp. prepared mustard
1 pkg. dry onion soup mix
2 cans (1 lb. 4 oz.) pork & beans

Brown hamburger, add remaining ingredients and simmer 15 minutes.

—Pat Bigler, Longview, Washington

ELEPHANT STEW

1 elephant (med. size)
2 rabbits (optional)
salt and pepper to taste

Cut elephant into bite-sized pieces (this takes about 2 months). Add enough gravy to cover. Cook over kerosene fire for 4 weeks at 465°. This will serve about 3,800 people. If more come than were expected, the 2 rabbits may be added, but do this *only if necessary,* as most people don't like hare in their stew.

Do your planning, organizing, telephoning, and desk work while you are alone in the house. When children come home from school, you are free to listen to them.

—Sarajane Steadley, Springfield, Virginia

Test of Love

To let no thought go unexpressed
    That might give someone pleasure;
To say no word I might regret
    in later hours of leisure;
To do the kindly little deed
    That makes life worth the living;
To overlook another's faults
    Nor fail to be forgiving;
To strive to leave each task well done
    And make a joy of duty;
Unceasingly to give God thanks
    For life, and love, and beauty;
To honor God and, loving Him,
    Love, as myself, my neighbor;
This, the high test of perfect love,
    The goal toward which we labor.

—Author unknown

FIVE-IN-ONE POT ROAST

Blade pot roast is one of the cheapest cuts of beef on the market, especially when on sale. Buy a large roast (at least 3 pounds) and cut it into small servings. The diagram below shows you how to cut it. Place in freezer ½ hour before cutting.

1. Steaks. Cut into two or three steaks, depending on size of pot roast. Broil.
2. Small pot roast. Tie together with string and braise, either in oven or on top of stove.
3. Stew meat. Cut in pieces.
4. Bones and extra meat from trimming. Use for soup stock. Cook over low heat with sufficient water to cover, at least 3 to 4 hours. Add carrots, onions, potatoes, and a can of tomatoes.
5. Fat. Hang this in the trees for the birds.

—Georgia Findling, Edmonds, Washington

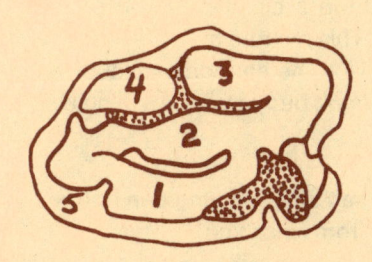

THREE-IN-ONE ROUND STEAK

Full-cut round steak is usually one of the better buys in the market. Look for it on sale. Buy large ones and then cut.

1. Top round. This may be broiled or used in any recipe calling for dry heat cookery.
2. Bottom round. This is less tender and should be used for Swiss steak.
3. Eye of the round. This is the least tender section of a full-cut round steak. Slice horizontally and quick fry for breakfast steaks.

—Georgia Findling, Edmonds, Washington

MAIN DISHES

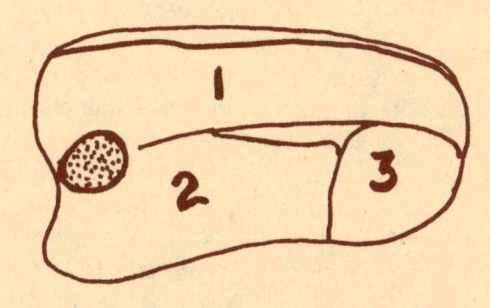

Homemaking Hints

Mark your plastic cleaning pail with fingernail polish to indicate your usual water levels (½ gal., 1 gal.) for scrubbing jobs.

— Elaine Yaeger, Stillwater, Minnesota

Wash your windows with vinegar and/or ammonia, then wipe dry with newspaper. Change the paper for each window.

— Evelyn Daniel, Sonora, California

Undiluted vinegar, used with a brush, will clean off water deposits on shower tile and glass.

— Patricia McCash, Frankfort, Michigan

Do all your major housecleaning and decorating projects before summer. Then, when your children are on vacation, you are, too.

— Ginny Defoe, Saginaw, Michigan

Put your hand inside a plastic bag to pick up a sticky or gooey item. Then invert the bag and tie it.

— Peggy Page, River Falls, Wisconsin

We learn from the Bible that the day before the Sabbath was called the day of preparation. Plan and work on Saturday, so that Sunday will truly be a day of rest.

— Merrily Yants, Liverpool, Texas

To stretch butter and margarine, whip it yourself. Put 1 lb. in a mixer bowl and beat until smooth. Add a little milk and beat, then twice more, add a little more milk and beat.

— Patricia McCash, Frankfort, Michigan

To clean your carpets, make a detergent of ½ cup ammonia to ½ gallon of water. Use a terry cloth rag and scrub gently in a circular motion over carpet. Repeat until clean. This mixture may be used in a rented carpet scrubber, also. The ammonia mixture will clean off old spots that won't budge with anything else.

— Elaine Yaeger, Stillwater, Minnesota

Sprinkle salt in your frying pan before frying meat, to prevent fat from splashing.

— Pauline Angotti, Willowdale, Ontario

I want to share with you some of the ways of living as a family that the Lord has shown us, and the wonderful results we have seen.

My husband and I have five children. Three of them are foster children and our own son is retarded but trainable. I am submitting several cookie recipes to the Aglow cookbook which are used by the children. I mention this fact because three of them are expected to bake one full batch of cookies or one cake per week for the family's use.

We have had many discussions about the children helping so that the mother has time to plan, purchase supplies, help her husband, supervise the house — things that require skill in management. At first, the children did not understand this idea, but as I persisted in pointing out the poor results and tensions that developed when I did more than my share, they recognized the importance of their helping.

I enjoy preparing the dinner table as a ministry in the Lord's name to whomever eats there by dressing it up with a bright centerpiece. This may be an arrangement of flowers, candles, a dried bouquet, or a heap of gourds.

We have several sets of inexpensive place mats and plates. In the fall we use green or orange mats, napkins to match and our orange and green plates. At Christmas, we have green mats, white napkins and plates, and put lots of red things in the centerpiece. In spring, we change to blue, or pink and white. This may sound complicated, but I find it easy and fun.

My husband is very happy about our quiet, orderly meal times. Precept by precept, the children have been trained how to hold their silverware properly eat nicely, and how to carry on a conversation.

Each dinner is followed by family devotions, in which we sing, read from the Bible, and pray. Everyone participates.

Each child has specific jobs to do. In addition, each one, regardless of age, makes his own bed. I took plenty of time teaching them to do their work well. I make them go back and do it again if it is unsatisfactory.

We have found that routine is the key to our successful family life. The retarded boy, and the foster children who had deep emotional problems when they came to us, have found peace and security in our home.

The Lord bless you and your family as He has ours.

—Emily Taylor, Juneau, Alaska

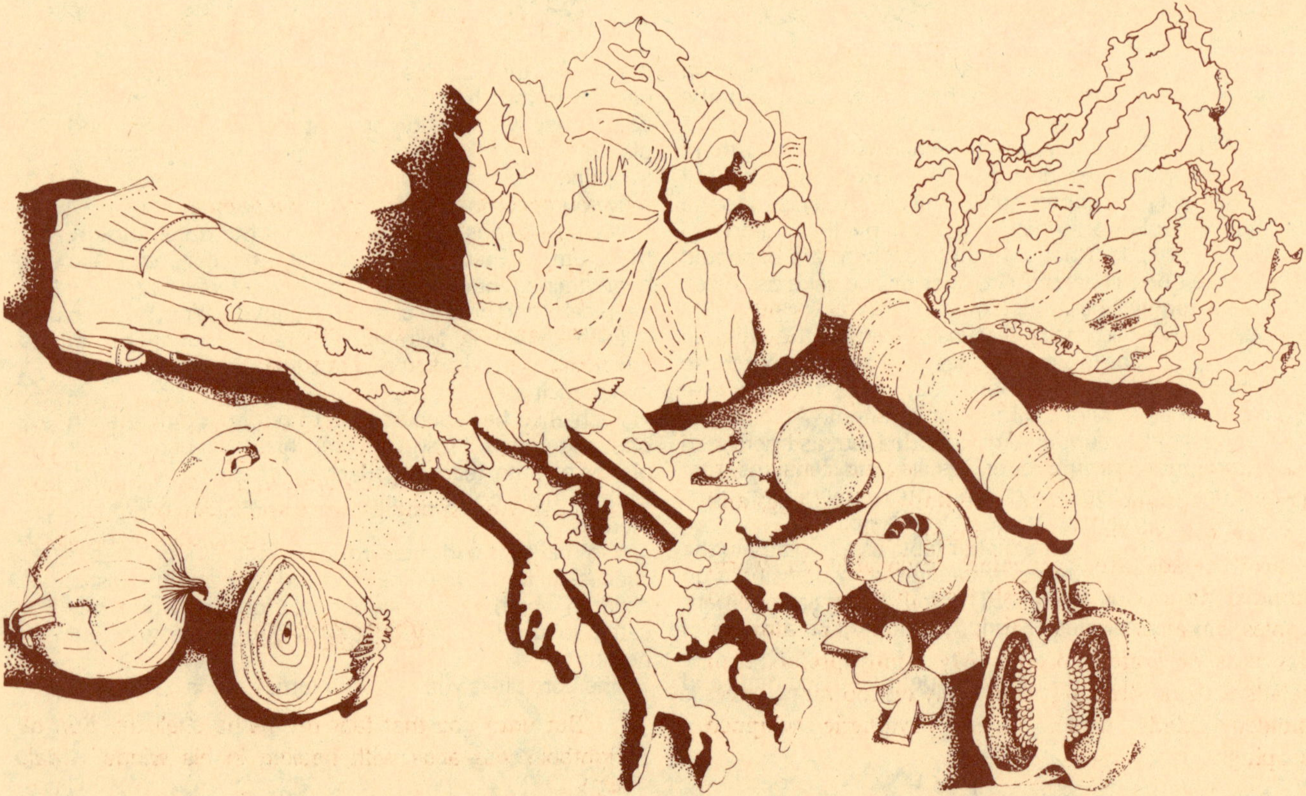

Salads and Vegetables

We feel that salads should be made of natural ingredients and play a significant role in the nutritional value of the entire meal. Generally speaking, they should be of the "green" variety, since research has proven our need for roughage.

Use different types of greens — various kinds of lettuce, spinach, endive, romaine, or Chinese cabbage. You may wish to add the usual diced celery, cucumber, and radishes, but be creative by adding other delicious ingredients, such as grated raw beets, raw broccoli, cauliflower, raw peas, and raw young asparagus tips. Try using sprouts. Garnish with hard-cooked eggs and sprinkle with sunflower or pumpkin seeds.

Fruit salads are particularly enjoyable on warm summer days. Use any fresh fruit in season — diced apples, bananas, oranges, grapes, melons. Try adding a few nuts or grated coconut. My family prefers fruit salads with no dressing. Don't rely on too many sweet molded salads which include synthetic whipped toppings.

FRESH VEGETABLE SALAD

If you use a glass bowl, the layers look very nice.

Serves: 6-8

1 small head lettuce, chopped
½ cup celery, sliced
⅓ cup green onions or chives, chopped
½ cup green pepper, sliced
1 pkg. (10 oz.) frozen peas, thawed
2 cups mayonnaise
½ cup Cheddar cheese, grated
bacon, either cooked and crumbled, or bits.

Layer lettuce, celery, onions, green pepper, peas in a bowl. Spread mayonnaise completely over the top, right to the sides of the bowl. Cover with plastic wrap. Let stand in refrigerator overnight, or at least 6 hours. Just before serving, sprinkle cheese and bacon over.

—Belva Miller, Cairo, Illinois

"But unto you that fear my name shall the Sun of righteousness arise with healing in his wings" (Mal. 4:2).

SALADS

SPINACH SALAD

Sliced hard-boiled eggs make a beautiful garnish.

Serves: 4-6

4 cups fresh spinach
1 Tbsp. olive oil
1 clove garlic, minced
3-4 fresh green onions, finely chopped
3-5 slices bacon
3 Tbsp. sugar
3 Tbsp. tarragon vinegar
1 egg

Wash and drain spinach. Remove stems and tear. Toss with olive oil in which garlic has set 15 minutes. Add onions. Saute bacon until crisp, saving grease. Add sugar and vinegar to grease and heat. Remove from stove, quickly add egg, and stir briskly. Pour over spinach then crumble bacon over this. Toss well. If wilted salad is desired, put into hot skillet and stir before serving.

—Margaret Rathkamp, San Antonio, Texas

"This is the day which the Lord hath made; we will rejoice and be glad in it" (Ps. 118:24).

84   SALADS

Teach your older children to plan ahead by having them write their activities on a handy family calendar. They will learn to fit in with other people's plans if they have to ask you a day ahead of time to drive them somewhere.

—Sarajane Steadley, Springfield, Virginia

CUCUMBER SALAD

A refreshingly different flavor is given by the mint.

Serves: 4

1 garlic clove, peeled
1 Tbsp. cider vinegar
1 cup yogurt
½ tsp. salt
dash pepper
2 Tbsp. olive oil
1½ Tbsp. fresh or dried mint, chopped or crumbled
1 med. cucumber, peeled, cut lengthwise into quarters, then into 2" strips

Mix ingredients together. Refrigerate, covered, until well chilled. Serve on lettuce leaves or from bowl.

—Mrs. Robert Melville, Spokane, Washington

MARINATED VEGETABLE SALAD

Keeps in refrigerator for ten days or more.

Serves: 8-10

1 can (1 lb.) whole kernel corn
   (white shoe peg variety, preferably)
1 can (1 lb.) tiny green peas
1 can (1 lb.) French style green beans
3 stalks celery, finely chopped
1 med. onion, finely chopped
1 small jar pimento
1 jar (4 oz.) sliced mushrooms

Drain and save juices from corn, peas, and beans. Combine all ingredients and mix together. Combine following ingredients in saucepan and heat until honey is mixed in:

scant ¼ cup honey
½ cup salad oil
1 tsp. salt
1 tsp. pepper
¾ cup vinegar
½ cup combined vegetable juices
1 tsp. paprika

Pour over vegetables and marinate in refrigerator at least 24 hours.

—Ellen Jones, Virginia Beach, Virginia

LENTIL CRUNCH SALAD

You might use this as a main dish for a summer meal. The lentils provide protein.

Serves: 4-6

1 cup lentils, cooked
1 apple, diced
1 cup cauliflower, finely sliced
½ cup walnut pieces
mayonnaise

Combine all ingredients with the mayonnaise thinned with plain yogurt or lemon juice. Serve on salad greens.

—Ruth Hicks, Seattle, Washington

BEET SALAD

The cheerful color and good crunch make this salad something extra.

Serves: 6-8

1 can (1 lb.) pickled beets, drained and cut in strips
1 can (1 lb.) julienne beets, drained
2 eggs, hard boiled and chopped
½ cup celery, chopped
1 tart apple, diced
1 small bag slivered almonds

Combine ingredients. Use mayonnaise and lemon juice for dressing.

—Ruth Lohrer, Seattle, Washington

"And these words, which I am commanding you this day, shall be (first) in your own mind and heart; (then) you shall whet and sharpen them, so as to make them penetrate, and teach and impress them diligently upon the (minds and) hearts of your children, and shall talk of them when you sit in your house, and when you walk by the way, and when you lie down and when you rise up" (Deut. 6:6-7 TAB).

COLESLAW FOR FREEZING

This makes a lot, but it keeps well, and may be refrozen.

1 medium to large head of cabbage
1 tsp. salt
1 carrot, grated
½ green pepper, chopped
1 cup vinegar
¼ cup water
1 tsp. mustard seed
1 tsp. celery seed
2 cups sugar (or part honey)

Mix cabbage and salt. Let stand one hour and squeeze out moisture. Add carrot and green pepper. While cabbage and salt are standing, mix remaining ingredients and boil one minute. Cool to lukewarm. Pour over cabbage mixture and mix gently. Pack and freeze. Thaw before serving.

—Nora Hoglund, Seattle, Washington

"Let not your heart be troubled: ye believe in God, believe also in me" (John 14:1).

BEAN SPROUT SALAD

Enjoyable with steak. Men have requested this recipe to give to their wives.

raw spinach
raw bean sprouts
¼ cup toasted sesame seeds
2 Tbsp. soy sauce
¼ cup lemon juice
¼ cup oil

Wash and shred raw spinach. Combine with equal amount of washed and chilled raw bean sprouts. Mix remaining ingredients in blender, then toss with spinach and bean sprouts.

—Nickalene Johnson, Poulsbo, Washington

Try preparing your dinner early in the morning. This leaves time to take a bath and freshen up for your husband before dinner. You will feel better, look better, and act better toward the whole family.

—Ruth Tilley, Florence, Kentucky

SPANISH TUNA SALAD

It's the olives that give a Spanish flair to this salad.

Serves: 6

½ large head leaf lettuce
3 stalks celery, cut in 1" pieces
2 Tbsp. onion, finely chopped
12 ripe olives
3 tomatoes, cut in wedges
1 can (6½ oz.) tuna, chunk style
1 egg, hard boiled and sliced.

Wash lettuce and drain on paper towel. Pull lettuce leaves into pieces. Place in large bowl. Add celery, onion, olives, and tomato. Toss well. Break up tuna and add to salad along with egg slices. Toss carefully. Refrigerate 1 hour, at least. Just before serving, pour oil and vinegar dressing over the salad. Toss very lightly to coat.

—Marsha Smith, Norfolk, Virginia

CARROT AND TUNA SALAD

This has a delightful variety of textures.

Serves: 4

1 cup raw carrot, grated
1 cup celery, diced
2 hard-cooked eggs, sliced
1 tsp. onion, grated
2 cans tuna, drained
1 cup mayonnaise
1 can shoestring potatoes

Mix together all ingredients except shoestring potatoes. Chill at least two hours. Just before serving stir in the potatoes.

—Betty Schumack, Lanesboro, Minnesota

''Then shall the righteous answer him, saying, Lord, when saw we thee an hungered, and fed thee? or thirsty, and gave thee drink? . . .

''And the King shall answer and say unto them, verily I say unto you, Inasmuch as ye have done it unto one of the least of these my brethren, ye have done it unto me'' (Matt. 25:37, 40).

THREE BEAN SALAD

A popular potluck or buffet dish.

1 can green beans
1 can wax beans
1 can kidney beans
½ cup green onions, minced
½ cup green pepper, minced
¾ cup sugar
½ cup salad oil
½ cup cider vinegar
¼ tsp. pepper
¼ tsp. salt

Combine ingredients. Refrigerate overnight.

—Gail Vaughan, Baytown, Texas

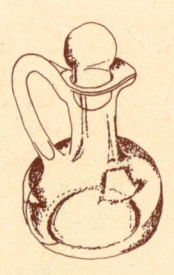

TURKEY SALAD SUPREME

Play the salad game: substitute chicken or tuna for turkey, and be creative with the seasonings.

Serves: 6-8

1½ cups turkey, cooked and diced
1 stalk celery, chopped
2 eggs, hard boiled and chopped
¼ lb. white seedless grapes, cut in halves
¼ cup nuts, chopped
1½ Tbsp. gelatin, unflavored
¼ cup cold water
½ cup turkey broth, hot
1 tsp. salt
¼ tsp. pepper
½ cup mayonnaise

Soak gelatin in cold water. Add hot turkey broth to dissolve. Cool. Combine celery, eggs, turkey, nuts, grapes, mayonnaise, and seasonings. Mix all ingredients together. Mold and chill.

—Virginia Stratton, Tacoma, Washington

LIL'S CHICKEN SALAD

Great to take to potlucks or for your own buffet.

Serves: 8-10

5 cups chicken, cooked, and diced
1 cup celery, chopped
2 cans (11 oz.) mandarin oranges
1 can (8 oz.) pineapple chunks
½ cup olives, chopped
1 cup cashews or walnuts

Mix all ingredients lightly with the following dressing:

½ pint cream, whipped (optional)
1 cup mayonnaise
1 Tbsp. curry powder
seasonings

Chill thoroughly. Serve in a pretty bowl or arrange on lettuce leaves. Garnish with olives and orange slices.

—Lillian Bingen, Bothell, Washington

TACO SALAD

Once you have had this, you will look forward to having it again.

1 med. onion, chopped
4 tomatoes, diced
1 avocado, diced
1 med. head lettuce, cut up
4 oz. Cheddar cheese, shredded
8 oz. French dressing
hot sauce to taste
1 lb. ground beef
1 can (15 oz.) kidney beans, drained
¼ tsp. salt
1 med. bag corn or taco chips, crushed

Brown ground beef in small amount of oil. Add kidney beans and salt; simmer 10 minutes. Mix onion, tomatoes, avocado, cheese, and lettuce. Toss with French dressing and hot sauce. Add corn chips and meat mixture (cooled) to rest of salad. You may put all ingredients together, except lettuce and corn chips, at least 7 hours ahead of serving.

—Virginia McGeary, Kent, Washington

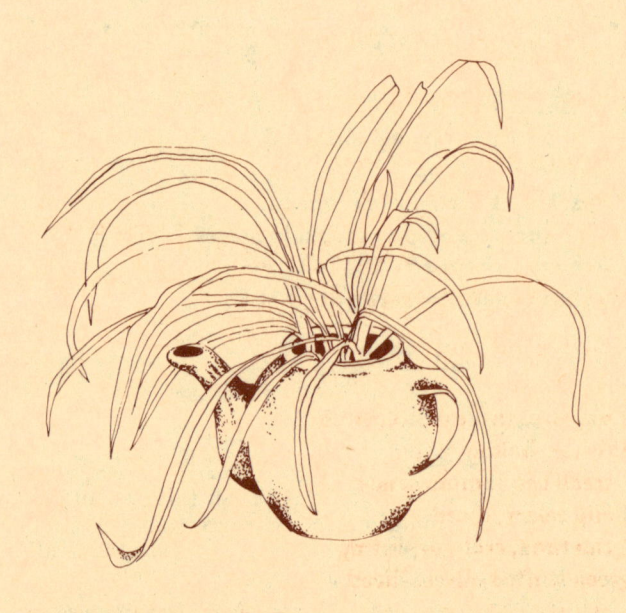

My life is but a weaving
Between my Lord and me;
I cannot choose the colors
He worketh steadily.
The dark threads are as needful
In the Weaver's skillful hand
As the threads of gold and silver
In the pattern He has planned.

—Author unknown

TOMATO ASPIC SALAD

Always a favorite.

Serves: 4-6

1 pkg. lemon-flavored gelatin
1¼ cups boiling water
1 small can tomato sauce
1 cup celery, diced
1 can tuna, crab, or shrimp
green stuffed olives, sliced

Add gelatin to boiling water and stir until gelatin is dissolved. Add tomato sauce and chill until syrupy. Add remaining ingredients. Put in 9" x 9" pan and refrigerate. Cut in squares to serve.

—Bernice Smith, Seattle, Washington

LIME SALAD

Brightens up any meal.

Serves: 8

2 pkgs. (3 oz.) lime gelatin
2 cups hot water
1 cup cream, whipped
½ cup salad dressing
¾ cup celery, chopped fine
¼ cup onion, chopped fine
1 carton (12 oz.) cottage cheese

Dissolve gelatin in hot water. Set aside until slightly set, then whip. Whip cream. Add remaining ingredients and mix together well. Pour into 9" x 11" pan and refrigerate until set.

—Naomi Homme, Anchorage, Alaska

"The man of few words and settled mind is wise; therefore, even a fool is thought to be wise when he is silent. It pays him to keep his mouth shut" (Prov. 17:27-28 TLB).

JIFFY CRANBERRY SALAD

Sanna says this is "really good."

Serves: 4-6

1 pkg. (3 oz.) black cherry-flavored gelatin
½ cup water
1 cup Sanna's Cooked Cranberry Sauce (see page 26)
½ cup nuts, chopped
1 cup or more plain yogurt
1 cup miniature marshmallows
1 banana, diced

Mix gelatin and water. Boil until thick and melted. Cool. Mix together cooled gelatin mixture, cranberry sauce, nuts, yogurt, marshmallows, and banana. Pour into a bowl or mold and chill.

—Sanna Le Van, Seward, Alaska

What we serve is not as important as **how** we serve it. The fruit of the earth is blessed by the fruit of the Spirit.

—Letitia Heil, Festus, Missouri

SUMMER SUPPER SALAD

You may use mixed vegetables in place of the beans and shrimp in place of the frankfurters, for variety.

Serves: 4-6

½ lb. elbow macaroni
1 can (1 lb.) kidney beans
4 beef frankfurters, sliced in rounds
½ cup sour cream
½ cup chili sauce
½ cup mayonnaise
¼ tsp. salt
dash pepper
1 tsp. prepared mustard
1 tsp. Worcestershire sauce

Cook macaroni as directed. Drain and rinse with cold water. Drain beans and discard juice. Mix sour cream, chili sauce, and mayonnaise, and mix well with beans. Mix beans and macaroni together and remaining ingredients. Cool. You may add finely chopped onion and celery and hard-cooked eggs.

—Mrs. Keith Tyner, Conrad, Montana

"You provide delicious food for me in the presence of my enemies. You have welcomed me as your guest; blessings overflow!" (Ps. 23:5 TLB).

DOUBLE RASPBERRY MOLD

Serves: 8-9

1 pkg. (6 oz.) raspberry gelatin
¼ cup jelly, any red flavor
3 cups boiling water
1 pkg. (10 oz.) frozen red raspberries
½ cup sour cream

Dissolve gelatin and jelly in boiling water; set aside ½ cup. Add frozen raspberries to the remaining gelatin mixture; stir until berries are separated and mixture thickens. Pour into a 1-qt. ring mold or metal bowl. Chill until firm — at least 4 hours. Meanwhile, blend reserved gelatin into sour cream and chill. Unmold ring. Stir sour cream mixture and serve with gelatin.

—Darlyne Holley, Moline, Illinois

HEAVENLY PINEAPPLE SALAD

Like sunshine on your plate.

1 pkg. (3 oz.) lemon gelatin
¾ cup pineapple juice
1 Tbsp. lemon juice
1¼ cups crushed pineapple
1 cup sharp Cheddar cheese, shredded
1 cup heavy cream, whipped

Dissolve lemon gelatin in 1 cup boiling water; add pineapple and lemon juices. Chill until slightly thick. Fold in 1 cup shredded cheese, pineapple, and whipped cream. Pour into 1½-qt. mold. Chill until set and unmold on fresh salad greens.

—Anne Fletcher, Virginia Beach, Virginia

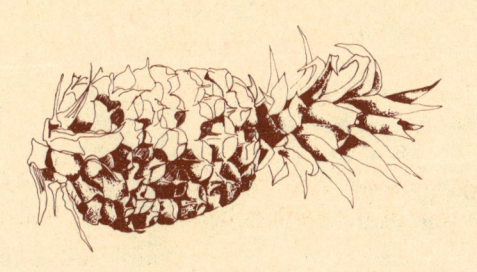

SALADS

FRENCH DRESSING

This is an old cherished recipe.

½ cup vinegar
½ cup oil
½ cup catsup
½ cup sugar
½ tsp. dry mustard
½ tsp. salt
½ tsp. paprika
2 Tbsp. grated onion
small clove garlic, mashed
1" piece cinnamon stick

Put all ingredients in a bottle and shake well.

—Evelyn Johnson, Coupeville, Washington

LOW CALORIE DRESSING

Two tablespoons of this dressing contain 25 calories and 2⅔ grams protein.

1 cup cottage cheese
1 can condensed tomato soup
1 Tbsp. sweet pickle relish
1 Tbsp. lemon juice
grated lemon rind (optional)

Put all ingredients in blender and blend. Chill. Stir before serving.

FRUIT SALAD DRESSING

A versatile dressing to be used on fruit or cooked vegetables. May be adapted for French or Thousand Island dressings, too.

1 cup sugar
1 tsp. celery seed
1 tsp. salt
2 tsp. dry mustard
sprinkle of paprika
1 Tbsp. grated onion
½ cup vinegar
2 cups salad oil

Mix all ingredients except oil in blender. Slowly add oil and blend well. Refrigerate. This can be made without blender, but will need to be stirred well before using. Will last as long as you want it to. Mix with mayonnaise, sour cream, or yogurt and add a little catsup for French dressing. Add pickles (chopped) and diced hard-boiled eggs to the French dressing for Thousand Island dressing.

—Ruth Hicks, Seattle, Washington

"But Jesus said, 'Let the children alone, and do not hinder them from coming to Me; for the kingdom of heaven belongs to such as these'" (Matt. 19:14 NASB).

WILLIAMSBURG DRESSING

This is good over fruit or greens.

½ cup vinegar
¼ cup sugar
¼ cup honey
1 tsp. dry mustard
1 tsp. paprika
1 tsp. celery seed
1 tsp. celery salt
1 tsp. onion juice
1 cup vegetable oil

Mix vinegar, sugar, honey, mustard, and paprika and boil for 3 minutes. Stir and cool. Add remaining ingredients. Put in bottle and store in refrigerator.

—Glenda Woodington, Portsmouth, Virginia

Pray for your children outloud before they leave for school and at bedtime. Teach them how to pray as soon as they are able. Let them pray for you, too. Out of the mouths of babes come words of wisdom.

— Mary Cass, Massillon, Ohio

TOSSED SALAD DRESSING

Once you start making your own salad dressings, you will think the bought ones have no "pizz-azz."

⅔ cup olive oil
⅓ cup vinegar—combine wine and cider vinegar for the best flavor
4 Tbsp. yogurt
2 tsp. honey
½ tsp. each: garlic powder, marjoram, basil
¼ tsp. dill
dash celery salt, salt, and pepper

Put above ingredients into a pint jar, shake, and chill.

—Yvonne G. Baker, Colorado Springs, Colorado

SUNSHINE SALAD

6 smiles (or more)
A few grins, but
   No giggles,
   No crabby words,
   No critical remarks.
Serve often to the man in your life.

—Submitted by Irene Doering, Puyallup, Washington

SALADS

BLENDER MAYONNAISE

As the blender does its work, you can allow one of the fruits of the Holy Spirit to be seen in you: patience. The result is well worth it!

1 egg
1 tsp. dry mustard
1 tsp. salt
dash cayenne pepper
1 tsp. sugar (optional)
1¼ cups salad oil
3 Tbsp. lemon juice
½ cup sour cream

    All ingredients should be at room temperature.
    Put egg, mustard, salt, cayenne, sugar, and ¼ cup oil in blender. Cover and blend until thoroughly combined. Remove lid with blender still running and *slowly* add ½ cup more oil, then lemon juice. Mix until well blended. Add the last ½ cup oil, slowly. Blend until thick. Stop the machine often to stir down the mayonnaise. When finished, stir in sour cream. Store in refrigerator.

—Margo Sterling, Churubusco, Mexico

    To remove gum from your child's hair, rub in peanut butter thoroughly, then wash.

—Nancy Smith, Dublin, Georgia

Kitchen Prayer

God bless my little kitchen,
I love its every nook.
Bless me as I do my work:
Wash pots and pans and cook.

May the meals that I prepare
Be seasoned from above
With Thy blessing and Thy grace,
But most of all, Thy love.

As we partake of earthly food,
The table for us spread,
We'll not forget to thank Thee, Lord,
Who gives us daily bread.

So bless my little kitchen, God,
And those who enter in.
May they find naught but joy and peace
And happiness therein.

—Submitted by Karen Axe, Kirkland, Washington

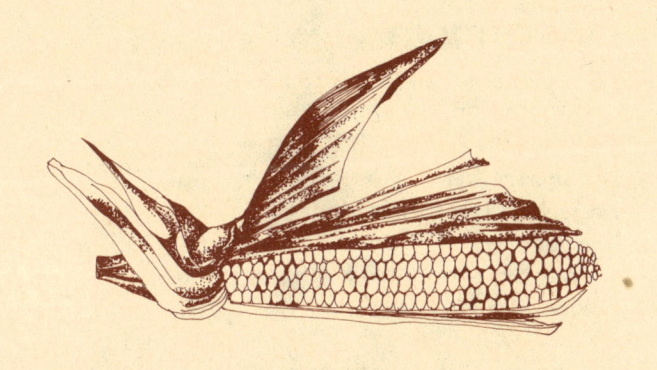

GREEN BEAN FLASH

A real time-saver. Keep the ingredients on your pantry shelf.

Oven: 350°   Serves: 6-8

3 cans cut green beans, drained
2 cans mushroom soup, undiluted
1 can fried onion rings

Place beans in a greased 2-qt. casserole dish. Salt and pepper to taste. Spread soup over beans. Spread onion rings on top. Bake about 15 minutes. For a smaller casserole use 1 can of beans, 1 can of soup, and as many fried onions as desired.

—Carolyn Bradley, McNeil, Arkansas

SUNSHINE CASSEROLE

Main dish or side dish — good as either one.

Oven: 300°   Serves 8-10

3 cups grated carrots
1 cup diced celery
1 cup soft bread crumbs
1 cup cubed mild Cheddar or Jack cheese
½ cup melted butter
½ cup chopped walnuts
1 cup chopped onion
2 eggs
1 tsp. salt

Combine ingredients. Place in large greased baking dish and bake covered, 40 minutes. Uncover and bake 5 minutes more.

—Carolyn Rasmussen, Bellevue, Washington

Once a week, we have a family night. We read and discuss the Bible together, play a game, have a special snack, or we all take a walk, have a picnic, etc. The sky is the limit for the kind of activity, as long as every member of the family participates and has a good time. We begin our family night with prayer and singing, and end it with a good-night prayer.

—Claudine Towle, Longview, Washington

APPLE CARROT STIRABOUT

If dinner is delayed, set aside, covered, and reheat when needed.

Serves: 6

4 Tbsp. butter
1 large onion, sliced
6 carrots, peeled and cut into 4 pieces each
2 large tart apples, unpeeled,
   but cored and sliced into ½ inch slices
¼ cup sugar
⅛ tsp. nutmeg
¼ tsp. salt
¼ tsp. dried sage leaves
⅛ tsp. cinnamon
¼ tsp. black pepper, freshly ground

Melt butter in large skillet. Add onion and saute until golden. Add carrots and cook 5 minutes longer. Add apples, sugar, and remaining ingredients. Mix well. Cover skillet and simmer over lowest heat for 40 minutes. Stir occasionally to keep from sticking.

—Marsha Smith, Norfolk, Virginia

SMOTHERED ASPARAGUS

Assemble the casserole ahead of time and put in the refrigerator. Bake ten minutes longer.

Oven: 350°   Serves: 4-6

1½ cups cracker crumbs
2 cans (1 lb.) asparagus, drained
4 cheese slices
1 can cream of mushroom soup
½ cup water

In a well-buttered 1½-qt. baking dish, spread crumbs evenly over the bottom. Arrange asparagus over crumbs, then a layer of cheese. Mix soup with water, spread half of mixture over cheese. Repeat with second layer of asparagus spears, then cover with remaining soup. Top with cheese. Bake for 30 minutes, until heated through and cheese is bubbly.

—Brenda Pittman, Portsmouth, Virginia

"I have learned how to get along happily whether I have much or little. I know how to live on almost nothing or with everything. I have learned the secret of contentment in every situation, whether it be a full stomach or hunger, plenty or want." (Phil. 4:11-12 TLB).

DUTCH BAKED CORN

Add a few pieces of cooked bacon, and this one becomes a main dish.

Oven: 350°   Serves: 4-6

4 ears fresh corn, cut off cob or 1 can (1 lb.) corn
1 Tbsp. butter
2 Tbsp. flour
1 cup milk
2 eggs, separated
2 tsp. sugar
1 tsp. salt
1 tsp. paprika
1 tsp. pepper

Melt the butter, mix with flour, pour milk in gradually, bring to boil. Add the corn and seasonings. Beat egg yolks and add to mixture. Beat egg whites until stiff, fold into mixture. Place in medium buttered casserole and bake 30 minutes.

—Sandra Stewart, Newark, Delaware

My soul was starving until I let Jesus cook the meals.
—Suzie Tharp, Dayton, Ohio

Recipe For Happiness

2 heaping cups of patience
2 handfuls of generosity
1 heart full of love
Dash of laughter
1 head full of understanding

Sprinkle, generously with kindness. Add plenty of faith. Mix well. Spread over a period of a lifetime and serve everybody you meet.

—Submitted by Betty Young, Vicksburg, Mississippi

STACKA-PACKA-ROO

Served with garlic bread and salad, this makes a complete meal, nutritious and filling.

Oven: 350°   Serves: 4-6

1 medium eggplant
4 oz. Monterey Jack or other cheese
1 can (16 oz.) tomato sauce
Parmesan cheese (optional)

Slice eggplant and dip in flour. Fry on both sides until eggplant softens and is brown. Place in medium greased casserole. Add cheese, then tomato sauce, then eggplant. Continue to stack in this manner. Bake 35 to 40 minutes.

—Margie Haton, Reno, Nevada

No Rinse Wall Cleaner

1 gal. hot water
1 cup ammonia
½ cup vinegar
¼ cup baking soda

Mix together and use for washing walls.

—Bernice Bell, Lansing, Michigan

VEGETABLES

VEGETABLE MEDLEY
A savory combination.

Oven: heat to 400°   Serves: 6

1 cup sliced onions, browned in a little butter
heart of 1 head of lettuce, cut in 1" cubes
1 cup cut string beans, frozen or fresh
1 cup celery, sliced
1 cup peas, frozen or fresh
1 cup carrots, cut in 1" strips
1 cup diced potatoes
⅓ cup butter
salt

Put onions in bottom of a large greased casserole dish. Layer each vegetable in turn dotting with butter. Cover tightly and bake for 20 minutes at 400°. Stir lightly to get juices around, season, and continue to bake for 30 minutes at 350°.

—Ann Thomas, Seattle, Washington

"Whatever happens to us is measured by the hand of God for our supreme good."

—Watchman Nee

POTATO PUFF
Light and tasty.

Oven: 350°   Serves: 4-6

2 cup mashed potatoes
2 Tbsp. Parmesan cheese, grated
1 Tbsp. melted butter
2 Tbsp. chopped onion
3 eggs, separated

Combine potatoes and cheese. Add butter and onion. Beat egg yolks and add to mixture. Beat whites until stiff. Fold into mixture. Turn into a deep, buttered 2-qt. casserole. Bake for 30 minutes or until a knife inserted in center comes out clean.

—Debby Heishman, Chambersburg, Pennsylvania

RECIPE FOR SOOTHING FUSSY BABIES
Hold crying infant or toddler close and sing Scripture songs. Soon both mother and child will be calmed.

—Sharon Ennis, Seward, Alaska

OOOOH-LA-LA POTATOES

A good main dish for a meatless meal. The cheese provides protein.

Oven: 300°   Serves: 6-8

6 medium potatoes
1 cup Cheddar cheese, shredded
6 Tbsp. butter
¾ cup sour cream
3 green onions, chopped
1 tsp. salt
¼ tsp. pepper

Cook potatoes in skins, cool. Peel and crumble with fork. Combine cheese and 4 Tbsp. butter in large saucepan; heat and stir until cheese is almost melted. Remove from heat; blend in sour cream, onions, salt, and pepper. Fold in potatoes. Spoon into greased 2-qt. casserole dish. Dot with 2 Tbsp. butter. Cover and bake for 25 minutes.

—Mary McCarty

RICE AND BROCCOLI

A delicious way to fix broccoli in the oven.

Oven: 350°   Serves: 4-6

1 cup cooked rice
2 pkgs. frozen broccoli, thawed
1 lg. onion, minced
3 Tbsp. butter
1 can cream of chicken soup
¾ cup milk
½ lb. cheese

Saute onion in butter until golden. Heat soup, milk, and cheese together until cheese is melted. Mix all ingredients and turn into baking dish. Bake 30-40 minutes.

—Sandy Stewart, Newark, Delaware

RUBY'S STUFFED PEPPERS

Our family has enjoyed many times of good fellowship as we ate a meal of stuffed peppers, cornbread, and salad.

Oven: 350°   Serves: 6

6 average green peppers
4 cups cooked rice
½ lb. ground beef
1 sm. onion, chopped
salt, pepper to taste
1 fresh tomato, cut in chunks
1 cup kernel corn, cooked or canned

Cut tops off peppers and scoop out seeds. In shallow, uncovered pan, steam peppers for 5 minutes in about 2" of water. In large mixing bowl, combine remaining ingredients lightly. Place peppers in medium sized baking-serving dish. Stuff pepper lightly. Dot tops with butter. Place any extra stuffing around peppers in baking dish. Bake 30 minutes or until ground beef is cooked well. Add catsup at table, if desired. To reheat, cover with aluminum foil and place in medium oven.

—Bobbie Taylor, Easton, Maryland

SPINACH SOUFFLE

This tastes so good that everyone turns into a Popeye when you serve it.

Oven: 350°   Serves: 6

2 cups cottage cheese
3 eggs, beaten
3 pkgs. frozen chopped spinach, thawed and drained
1½ cups grated Cheddar cheese
salt to taste

Mix cottage cheese and eggs with spoon in bowl. Add remaining ingredients, saving a little Cheddar cheese to sprinkle on top. Pour in greased 9" x 11" baking dish. Sprinkle cheese on top. Bake 30 to 45 minutes until set.

—Carol Dicus, Walla Walla, Washington

"It doesn't matter, really, how great the pressure lies. See that it never comes between you and the Lord. Then, the greater the pressure, the more it presses you to His breast."

—J. Hudson Taylor

VEGETABLES

BEST EVER SPINACH AND RICE

Each serving has 10 grams of usable protein.

Oven: 350°   Serves: 4

¾ cup cooked brown rice
½ cup grated cheese
1 lb. fresh spinach, chopped
2 eggs, beaten
2 Tbsp. parsley, chopped
½ tsp. salt
¼ tsp. pepper
2 Tbsp. wheat germ
1 Tbsp. margarine or butter, melted

Combine cooked rice and cheese. Combine eggs, parsley, salt, and pepper. Add the two mixtures together and stir in raw spinach. Pour into oiled casserole. Top with wheat germ which has been mixed with melted butter. Bake for 35 minutes.

—Ruth Hicks, Seattle, Washington

"Fire goes out for lack of fuel, and tensions disappear when gossip stops" (Prov. 26:20 TLB).

"Speak not, I passionately entreat thee, till thy thought have silently matured itself. Out of silence comes thy strength. 'Speech is silvern; silence is golden. Speech is human; silence is divine.'"

—Carlyle

VEGETABLE DIP

Raw vegetables contain lots of the vitamins, minerals, and fiber essential to good health.

⅔ cup mayonnaise
⅔ cup sour cream
1 Tbsp. dry green onions
1 Tbsp. parsley flakes
1 tsp. dill weed
1 tsp. seasoning salt
½ tsp. Worcestershire sauce
1 tsp. Accent
2 drops Tabasco

Blend all ingredients and serve as dip for raw vegetables: carrots, celery, tomatoes, cauliflower, etc.

—Brenda Pittman, Portsmouth, Virginia

ITALIANO SQUASH

May be frozen for future use.

                Oven: broil   Serves: 4-6

1½ cups tomato sauce
1 tsp. oregano
1 tsp. garlic salt
2 cups of 1" slices of zucchini,
   vegetable marrow, or crookneck squash
2 Tbsp. Romano or Parmesan cheese
1 Tbsp. bread crumbs

    Combine tomato sauce, oregano, and garlic salt in medium sauce pan. Add squash and cook 10 minutes. Put in medium baking dish. Combine cheese and bread crumbs and sprinkle on top. Broil 3 minutes.

                —Helen Dale, Beeton, Ontario, Canada

If we change the "d" in disappointment to an "H", we find our problem changed to His appointment."

        —Submitted by Marilyn Cecil, Watertown, New York

ESCALLOPED ZUCCHINI

One good way to remove an overload of zucchini in the summer.

                Oven: 325°   Serves: 4-6

1 lb. zucchini, peeled and sliced
1 can whole kernel or cream style corn
1 egg, slightly beaten
4 Tbsp. cream with whole kernel corn or 1 Tbsp. cream with cream style corn
grated cheese

    Cook squash, drain, and mash. Add other ingredients. Season and put in baking dish. Top with grated cheese. Bake 45 minutes.

                —Evelyn Johnson, Coupeville, Washington

VEGETABLES

SOUTHERN SWEETIES

There are lots of vitamins in sweet potatoes.

Oven: 350° Serves: 6-8

6 medium fresh, or 2 cans, sweet potatoes
¼ cup butter
1 tsp. vanilla
2 eggs
½ tsp. salt
½ tsp. cinnamon

Boil fresh potatoes until tender, skin. If canned potatoes are used, heat them well in the liquid from the can. Drain.

Put potatoes and the rest of the ingredients in a mixing bowl and beat until fluffy. Any strings from the potatoes will stay on the beaters. Pour into a buttered casserole and top with a mixture of ¼ cup melted butter, ¾ cup brown sugar, and ½ cup pecans. Bake 30 minutes.

—Sylvia Sistrunk, Jackson, Mississippi

LO-CAL CABBAGE

Half a bouillon cube added to the cooking water eliminates the need for salting vegetables.

1 small head of cabbage, cut in thin wedges
2 stalks celery, cut up
1 green pepper, seeded and sliced

Put these in a pan with about 1 cup water and 1 cube of chicken bouillon. Cook until tender. Add sliced cheese on top, cover, and let the cheese melt.

—Barbara Kehoe, Muncie, Indiana

"Let him have all your worries and cares, for he is always thinking about you and watching everything that concerns you" (1 Pet. 5:7 TLB).

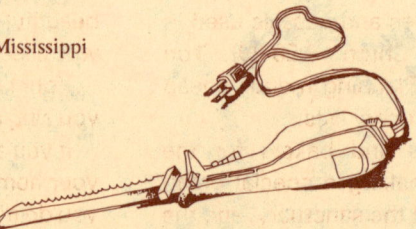

Serve the Lord With Gladness

You will probably agree that your husband should be a "priest" in your home, taking the leadership in both spiritual and practical matters. Have you ever thought that you, as a Christian wife, can be likened to a Levite, assisting the priest?

Let's look at some of the duties of the Levites and see how they compare with your duties at home:

1. They were the gatekeepers and opened the gates every morning (1 Chron. 9:26-27). Do you keep guard over what is allowed to enter your children's minds through TV and their lives, through friends?

2. They were the supply keepers and shoppers. They looked after the supplies and vessels used in sacrifices and worship (1 Chron. 9:28-29). You probably do the shopping. Planning menus ahead helps in making out thrifty grocery lists.

3. They were the cooks and bakers for the tabernacle. This included making a special bread for the table of showbread in the sanctuary, and the making of flat cakes for grain offerings (1 Chron. 9:31-32). Do you take time to prepare wholesome food to ensure your family's well being?

4. They were the makers of incense for the golden altar (1 Chron. 9:30). The burning of incense is a picture of prayer ascending up to the throne of God. Is your home a "house of prayer"? Do you make it easy for your family to have meaningful times of prayer together?

5. They were the musicians for the house of God (1 Chron. 9:33). Some Levites were trained as singers; others played instruments (2 Chron. 5:12). They were to praise God in song every morning and evening (1 Chron. 23:30). When Solomon's temple was dedicated, a Levite choir and orchestra gave beautiful musical praise to God, and the Temple was filled with the glory of God (2 Chron. 5:12-14).

Your home may also be filled with God's glory as you sing and give praise to Him.

If you are convinced that the work you do around your home is for the glory of God, try singing while you do it! Learn to serve the Lord with gladness.

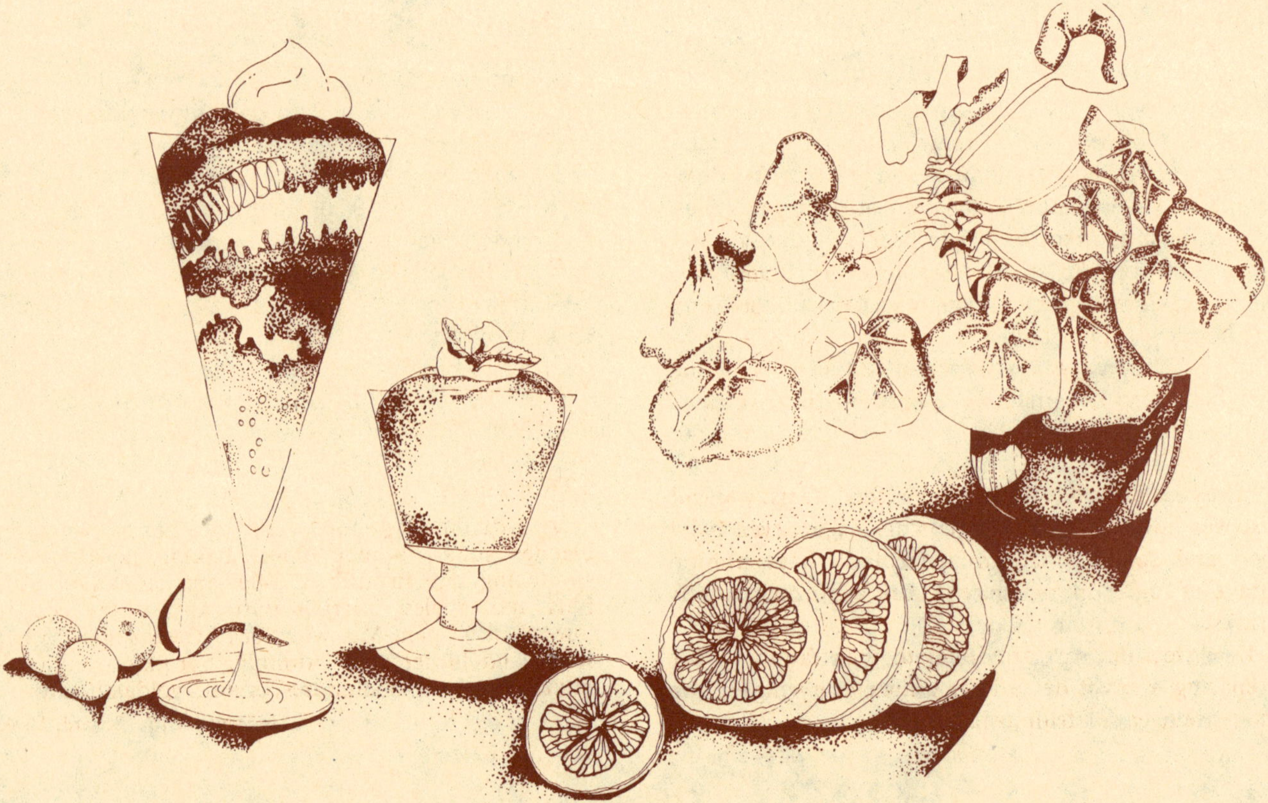

Desserts

I used to feel that I had to prepare a dessert every day for dinner to keep my family happy. Since I gave them dessert every day, they came to expect it.

Dr. John Yudkin of London University claims that the average person in our western world eats more than one hundred pounds of refined sugar a year — two pounds or more a week! After considerable research, he and his colleagues feel that refined sugar may be a significant factor in heart disease, ulcers, and other diseases.

If you read labels of store-bought food items, you will discover how many of them contain sugar, even baby food and soups. Children particularly have a high intake of sugar, from sugared breakfast cereals to soft drinks.

Don't feel that you are depriving your family by not preparing a sweet dessert for dinner every night. Get them use to eating fruit instead.

APPLE NUT DESSERT

After trying this once, your family will want it often.

Oven: 400°   Serves: 4-6

1 cup sugar
¾ cup flour
2 tsp. baking powder
1 Tbsp. shortening
½ cup evaporated milk
1 tsp. vanilla
dash cinnamon
½ cup nuts, broken
3 cups apples, sliced
2 Tbsp. brown sugar
⅓ cup flour
2 Tbsp. butter

In 2-qt. mixing bowl, cut together with pastry blender sugar, ¾ cup flour, baking powder, and shortening. Stir in milk, vanilla, and cinnamon. Add nuts and apples, stirring until apples are coated. Spread in 9" pan. Mix with fork brown sugar, ⅓ cup flour, and butter until crumbly. Sprinkle over apple mixture. Bake 30-35 minutes, or until golden brown.

—Sanna LeVan, Seward, Alaska

CHOCOLATE BREAD PUDDING

An old Vermont recipe.

Oven: 375°   Serves: 4-6

4 cups milk
2 cups bread crumbs
1 cup sugar
2 Tbsp. cocoa
dash of salt
2 eggs
1 tsp. vanilla
½ tsp. cinnamon

Warm the milk, add bread crumbs. Mix together sugar, cocoa, and salt. Beat eggs, vanilla, cinnamon together and combine with milk and sugar mixture. Bake 1 hour. Serve warm or cold.

—Ruth Wells, Saxtons River, Vermont

"If Jesus Christ be God and died for me, then no sacrifice can be too great for me to make for Him."

— C. T. Studd

"Do you not know that your body is the temple — the very sanctuary — of the Holy Spirit Who lives within you, Whom you have received (as a Gift) from God? You are not your own, you were bought for a price — purchased with a preciousness and paid for, made His own. So then, honor God and bring glory to Him in your body" (1 Cor. 6:19-20 TAB).

CLERGYMAN'S COBBLER

Will serve four normal people or one hungry preacher and two friends.

Oven: 350°

½ cup butter
1 cup flour
1 cup sugar
1 cup milk
1 can (large) peaches, drained

Melt butter in loaf pan. Mix together flour and sugar. To the melted butter add milk and sugar-flour mixture. Mix well. Add drained peaches, stir lightly. Bake 1 hour. Serve hot.

—Joan Driesen, Vicksburg, Missouri

BUSY DAY COBBLER

This is delicious hot or cold, so don't worry if you make it at the last minute.

Oven: 400°   Serves: 6-8

4-6 cups fruit: apples, apricots, blueberries, cherries, peaches, or blackberries
½ cup sugar
1 cup water
1 egg, beaten
½ tsp. salt
1 tsp. baking powder
1 cup sugar or less depending on sweetness of fruit
1 cup flour
⅓ cup butter, melted

Place fruit in a 9"x13" baking pan. Combine ½ cup sugar and water and pour over fruit. Mix egg, salt, baking powder, sugar, and flour together. Spread over fruit. Pour butter over top. Bake 30 minutes or until golden brown.

—Margaret Knowling, Bothell, Washington

Our women's Bible study group often has social occasions which include our husbands and usually our children. We have had a game night, where each family has brought their favorite game and a snack to share with the group. On Halloween night, we had a "Hallelujah Night" and sponsored a hayride and hot dog roast. Valentine's Day was used for a "Jesus Loves You" party. We made valentines inscribed with love Scriptures, played games, snacked, and talked. We are planning a progressive supper for couples in our group.

—Cari Mickey, Wellsboro, Pennsylvania

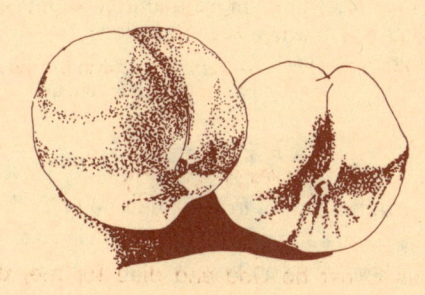

LEMON TWIN

This pretty dessert ends up having cake on top and pudding on the bottom.

Oven: 350°   Serves: 4-6

2 Tbsp. butter
1 cup sugar
2 Tbsp. flour, sifted
4 Tbsp. lemon juice or
   juice and grated rind of 1 large lemon
2 egg yolks, beaten
1 cup milk
2 egg whites, stiffly beaten

Cream butter and sugar. Add flour, lemon juice, and egg yolks. Mix and stir in milk and egg whites. Pour in lightly buttered baking dish and place in pan of water. Bake 35-40 minutes.

—Doris Johnson, Colusa, California

"Be beautiful inside, in your hearts, with the lasting charm of a gentle and quiet spirit which is so precious to God. That kind of deep beauty was seen in the saintly women of old, who trusted God and fitted in with their husbands' plans" (1 Pet. 3:4-5 TLB).

"The sweet peace of God bears the outward token of resignation. When the Holy Spirit dwells within us, everything seems bright.

"Everything may not be exactly as we would wish it, but we accept all with a good grace. For instance, some change in our household or mode of living upsets us. If God is with us, He will whisper, 'Yield cheerfully thy will; in a little while all will be forgotten.'

"Some command or employment wounds our pride; if God is with us, He will say to us, 'Be submissive, and I will come to thine aid.' "

—Submitted by Nancy Rawley, Kirkland, Washington

APPLE PUDDING

The flavor of the apples is important in giving this dessert either a tart or a milder taste.

Oven: 325°

2 cups sugar
2 eggs
½ cup shortening or butter, softened
2 tsp. vanilla
2 cups flour
1 tsp. cinnamon
1 tsp. nutmeg
1½ tsp. soda
½ tsp. salt
6 large apples, diced
2 cups chopped nuts

Mix all ingredients together. Put into two 9" pie pans. Bake 35-45 minutes.

—Doris Johnson, Colusa, California

SMOOTHIE RAISIN PIE

try

This recipe is at least three generations old! The pie is quite rich, so don't cut the pieces very big.

Oven: Heat to 450°   Yield: 1-9" pie

1 cup flour
½ tsp. salt
⅓ cup shortening
2-3 Tbsp. cold water
3 eggs, slightly beaten
1¼ cups sugar
½ tsp. salt
1 tsp. cinnamon
¼ tsp. cloves
1½ cups sour cream
1½ cups raisins

Make a pastry from flour, salt, shortening, and water. Roll out, and line pan, forming a fluted, standing rim.

Combine eggs, sugar, salt, cinnamon, and cloves. Blend in sour cream and raisins. Pour into pan.

Bake in hot oven for 10 minutes, then lower oven heat to 325° and continue baking for 20-25 more minutes or until a knife inserted in the filling comes out clean.

—Juanita Reese, Hermitage, Missouri

DESSERTS

STRAWBERRY CHEESE CAKE

The red and white color makes this a pretty Christmas dessert.

Oven: 350°   Yield: 2 pies

4 pkgs. (3 oz.) cream cheese
1½ cups sour cream
3 eggs, slightly beaten
¾ cup sugar
1½ tsp. vanilla
2 pkgs. frozen strawberries
2 Tbsp. cornstarch
juice from strawberries

Combine cream cheese, sour cream, eggs, sugar, and vanilla and whip at medium speed for 4 minutes. Pour cheese mixture into pie pans lined with graham cracker crusts. Bake 30 minutes. Top should be golden brown. Cool before topping with glaze. To make glaze, thaw and drain strawberries. Add cornstarch to juice from berries and heat slowly until mixture thickens. Arrange fruit on top of cheese cake, pour thickened juice mixture over the top. Refrigerate until ready to serve. Have at room temperature before serving or cheese tends to crumble.

—Beverly McFadden, Bettendorf, Illinois

QUICKY CHEESE CAKES

There is something appealing about little individual desserts for a change.

Oven: 375°   Serves: 18

18 vanilla wafers
2 eggs
½ cup sugar
2 pkgs. (8 oz.) cream cheese
2 tsp. vanilla
1 can (22 oz.) pie filling (cherry or blueberry)

Place 18 paper cupcake liners in muffin tins. Put one wafer in each. Mix eggs, sugar, cream cheese, and vanilla together at medium speed for 5 minutes. Spoon into liners until ¾ full. Bake 12 to 15 minutes. Let cool, then spoon on pie filling.

—Pearl Lovell, Phoenix, Arizona

"She is a woman of strength and dignity, and has no fear of old age. When she speaks, her words are wise, and kindness is the rule for everything she says. She watches carefully all that goes on throughout her household, and is never lazy" (Prov. 31:25-27 TLB).

MINCEMEAT PIE

An easy version of old-time mincemeat.

Oven: 350°

¼ lb. ground beef
3 medium cooking apples,
   peeled and finely chopped
¾ cup dark brown sugar
½ cup seedless raisins
½ cup apple juice or cider
1 Tbsp. cider vinegar
1½ tsp. cinnamon
1 tsp. salt
½ tsp. ground cloves
¼ cup brandy (optional)

In large saucepan over medium high heat, heat to boiling all ingredients except brandy, stirring occasionally. Reduce heat to low; cover and simmer 30 minutes. Stir in brandy, if used. Place in favorite pie crust and bake for 30 minutes or until crust is golden brown.

—Sandy Parrott, Moline, Illinois

Jesus is the sweetest name I know!

MIRACLE PIE

This pie makes its own crust, filling, and topping.

Oven: 400°

4 eggs
2 cups milk
½ cup sugar
½ cup Bisquick
1 tsp. vanilla
3 Tbsp. butter
½ cup coconut
dash of nutmeg

Put all ingredients in blender and blend for 15 seconds. Pour into buttered pie pan. Bake 25-30 minutes.

—Darlene Smith, Salina, Kansas

DESSERTS   115

PINK SURPRISE APPLE PIE

It's as "easy as pie."

1 pie crust
1 can (1 lb.) crushed pineapple, drained
3-4 apples, grated
½ cup whipping cream, whipped
½ carton (8 oz.) raspberry yogurt

Fill pie crust with fruit. Combine whipped cream and yogurt and spread over fruit. Chill 3 hours.

—Jacqui Dunham, Santa Cruz, California

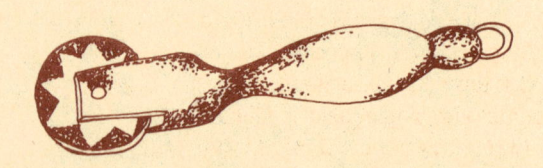

For a flaky pie crust, try adding milk instead of water.

— Nancy Smith, Dublin, Georgia

YOGURT CREAM PIE

A delectably smooth cream pie.

Oven: 375°

Crust:
1¾ cups graham cracker crumbs
¼ cup walnuts, chopped
½ tsp. cinnamon
½ cup butter, melted

Combine all ingredients and press on bottom and sides of 9" pie pan. Bake 8 minutes.

2 cups yogurt, plain or vanilla
1 cup sour cream
1 cup vanilla ice cream
1 tsp. vanilla or almond flavoring
2 Tbsp. honey
½ tsp. salt
2 envelopes gelatin, unflavored, softened in 3 Tbsp. cold water

In bowl combine yogurt, sour cream, and ice cream. Over low heat dissolve gelatin with honey, salt, and vanilla. Cool. Add to yogurt mixture. Pour into crust and chill 5-6 hours.

—Marcia May, Kirkland, Washington

FRENCH PASTRY

A foolproof, tender pastry.

3 cups flour
1 cup + 1½ Tbsp. shortening
1½ tsp. salt
1 egg
⅓ cup ice water
1 tsp. cider vinegar

    Cut together flour, shortening, and salt. In separate bowl beat the egg, water, and vinegar together. Add to flour mixture. Stir until the pastry forms into a ball.

—Alsea Britton, Lewis, Kansas

"So don't worry at all about having enough food and clothing. Why be like the heathen? . . . But your heavenly Father already knows perfectly well that you need them, and he will give them to you if you give him first place in your life and live as he wants you to" (Matt. 6:31-33 TLB).

A big pinch of salt added to sour fruits while cooking will greatly reduce the quantity of sugar needed to sweeten them.

—Elizabeth Van Dyk, Cave Junction, Oregon

Success

Once upon a time I planned to be
    An artist of celebrity,
A song I thought to write one day,
    And all the world would homage pay.
I longed to write a noted book.
    But what I did was learn to cook.
For life with single tasks is filled
    And I have done not what I willed,
Yet when I see boys' hungry eyes,
    I'm glad I make good apple pies!

—Submitted by Betty Schumack, Lanesboro, Minnesota

DESSERTS

LAYERED APPLESAUCE

Serves: 6

½ cup margarine
2 cups rolled oats
1 Tbsp. brown sugar
1 can (2 cups) applesauce
1 cup nuts

Melt margarine in skillet. Add oats, toasting over medium heat, stirring constantly until golden brown. Stir in brown sugar and nuts. In individual bowls, alternate layers of applesauce and oat mixture. To keep dessert from becoming soggy, layer *just* before serving.

—Hazel Tappy, Shenandoah, Virginia

BAKED PINEAPPLE CUSTARD

A nice dessert to cook with an oven meal.

Oven: 350°   Serves: 6

½ cup sugar
½ stick margarine, melted
4 slices bread, crumbled
1 can (16 oz.) crushed pineapple, not drained
2 eggs, beaten

Mix all ingredients together. Put in greased 1-qt. casserole and bake 30 minutes.

—Mary Shank, Mechanicsburg, Pennsylvania

CUP CUSTARD

A simple and nourishing dessert.

Oven: 350°   Serves: 4

2 cups milk, scalded
3 eggs
3 Tbsp. sugar
⅛ tsp. salt
1 tsp. vanilla

Scald milk and set aside to cool. Beat eggs. Add sugar, salt, and vanilla. Stir in cooled milk. Pour into custard cups. Bake in pan of water (¾" deep) until firm, about ½ hour.

—Mrs. Richard Marquette, Lincoln, Nebraska

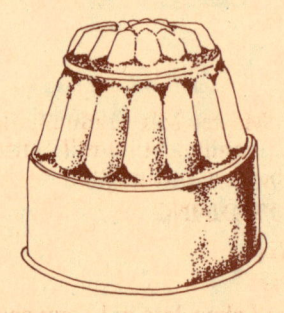

MASTER MIX FOR PUDDINGS OR CREAM PIES

Costs less than the packaged kind you buy.

Yield: 2 cups

¾ cup sugar
3⅓ cups instant non-fat dry milk
¾ cup cornstarch
½ tsp. salt

Combine ingredients and store in tightly covered container in a cool, dry place. Stir mix before using. Use this Master Mix for the following two pudding recipes.

VANILLA PUDDING

1 cup Master Mix
2 cups cold water
1 tsp. butter
½ tsp. vanilla

Add water to Master Mix gradually. Bring to a boil. Add butter and vanilla. Stir until butter melts. Pour into serving dishes and refrigerate.

CHOCOLATE PUDDING

1 cup master Mix
2 cups cold water
1 oz. unsweetened chocolate or ¼ cup cocoa
½ tsp. vanilla

Add water to Master Mix gradually. Bring to a boil. Add chocolate or cocoa. Stir in vanilla.

—Sandie Gotsch, Oakland, Missouri

Hindering Weights

"The things which hinder are not necessarily low or vulgar. They may be in themselves noble things, intellectual things, beautiful things. But if our participation in any of these dims our vision of the ultimate goal in the purpose of God, holds us in our running, makes our going less determined and steady, they become weights and hinder."

—G. Campbell Morgan

FRUIT GEL

The real thing; nothing artificial.

2 Tbsp. plain gelatin
1 cup cold water
⅔ cup honey
¼ cup fresh-squeezed lemon juice
2 cups any fruit juice
   (orange or pineapple is especially good)
One or two spoonfuls beet juice for coloring (optional)

   In saucepan, mix gelatin and water. Add honey, and heat to dissolve. Add juices. Apple juice is good, but sweeter; cut down on the honey. For a lemon gelatin, use 1½ cups apple juice and juice of 2 limes and 1 lemon.

—Mrs. Robert Melville, Spokane, Washington

POLKA DOT JELLO

Use different colors to fit the season: red for Christmas, yellow for summer, orange for fall.

1 pkg. (3 oz.) lemon gelatin
1 cup crushed pineapple
1 cup diced red-skinned apples
½ cup nuts
½ cup small marshmallows

   When gelatin thickens, add other ingredients. Place in refrigerator until set.

—Hilda Wenger, Manheim, Pennsylvania

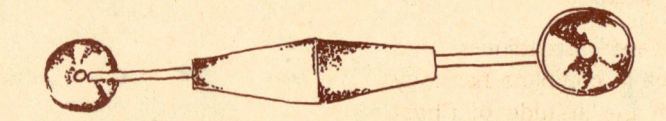

HEAVENLY RICE PUDDING

This is unusual because it is cooked on top of the stove.

1 qt. milk
1 orange
½ cup white rice, uncooked
½ cup sugar
½ tsp. salt
2 egg yolks
1 cup milk
1 tsp. vanilla

   Scald milk with spiral of orange peel. Add rice, sugar, salt, and cook gently 45 minutes. Blend egg yolks with 1 cup milk and slowly stir into hot rice mixture. Continue simmering for 20 minutes. Add vanilla. To serve, garnish with orange sections.

—Noretta Lake, Hamilton, Ohio

"May God who gives patience, steadiness, and encouragement help you to live in complete harmony with each other — each with the attitude of Christ toward the other. And then all of us can praise the Lord together with one voice, giving glory to God, the Father of our Lord Jesus Christ" (Rom. 15:5-6 TLB).

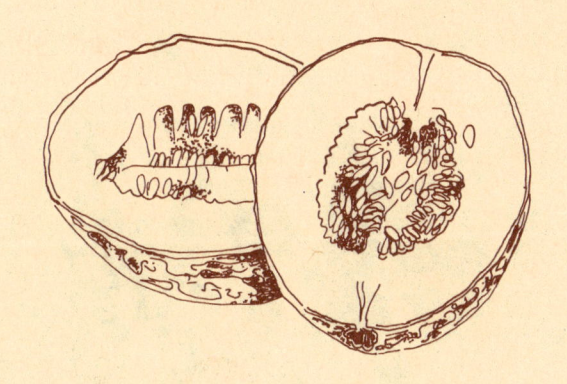

FRUIT FREEZE

A summer "special" but don't limit yourself to one season when serving this dessert.

2 cans (6 oz.) frozen orange juice
1 can (13¼ oz.) crushed pineapple
4 Tbsp. lemon juice
3 ripe bananas, mashed
1 cup gingerale
¾ cup sugar

Mix together and freeze. Remove 10 minutes before serving.

—Mrs. Richard Marquette, Lincoln, Nebraska

"You wives, submit yourselves to your husbands, for that is what the Lord has planned for you. And you husbands must be loving kind to your wives and not bitter against them, nor harsh. You children must always obey your fathers and mothers, for that pleases the Lord. Fathers, don't scold your children so much that they become discouraged and quit trying" (Col. 3:18-21 TLB).

BLUEBERRY REFRIGERATOR PIE

Either fresh or frozen blueberries can be used.

2 cups blueberries
½ cup water
⅔ cup sugar
pinch of salt
1 Tbsp. lemon juice
3 Tbsp. cornstarch mixed with a little water to make a paste

Cook fresh berries in water for a few minutes. Add water to frozen berries and let thaw. Mix sugar, salt, lemon juice, and cornstarch. Cook together until thick. Add blueberries, and cook a few more minutes.

Pour into baked graham cracker pie shell. Chill.

—Beth Hawkins, Tacoma, Washington

SHAKE-A-JELLO

The kids love to do the shaking. Check the fit of the cover on the bowl, first.

1 pkg. (3 oz.) gelatin
1 cup boiling water
6-8 ice cubes
1 cup ice cream

Put all in bowl with tight-fitting cover and shake until cubes melt. Remove lid, pour into serving dishes and refrigerate until firm (15-20 minutes).

APPLE CRUNCH

Rhubarb, cut up, can be substituted for the apples in this recipe.

Oven: 350°

1 cup flour
¾ cup rolled oats
1 cup brown sugar
1 tsp. cinnamon
½ cup butter, melted
4 cups sliced apples
1 cup sugar
2 Tbsp. cornstarch
1 cup water
1 tsp. vanilla

Mix flour, rolled oats, brown sugar, cinnamon, and melted butter until crumbly. Press half into greased 9" pan. Cover with apples.

Combine sugar, cornstarch, water, and vanilla and cook until clear and thick. Pour over fruit. Top with remaining crumbs. Bake 1 hour.

—Sandy Parrott, Moline, Illinois

DESSERTS

PUMPKIN TORTE

Peter the Pumpkin-eater never had it this good!

Oven: 350°   Serves: 8

24 (2¼ cups) graham crackers, crushed
⅓ cup sugar
½ cup butter, melted
2 eggs, beaten
¾ cup sugar
1 pkg. (8 oz.) cream cheese
2 cups pumpkin, canned
½ cup sugar
½ tsp. salt
3 egg yolks
½ cup milk
1 Tbsp. cinnamon
1 envelope plain gelatin, soaked in ¼ cup cold water
3 egg whites
¼ cup sugar
½ pt. whipping cream

  Mix butter with ⅓ cup sugar and graham crackers. Press into 9" x 13" pan.
  Mix eggs, ¾ cup sugar, cream cheese, pour over crust, and bake for 20 minutes.
  Cook pumpkin, ½ cup sugar, salt, egg yolks, milk, and cinnamon until mixture thickens. Remove from heat and add softened gelatin. Cool. Beat egg whites, slowly adding ¼ cup sugar. Fold into pumpkin mixture and pour over crust. Chill for several hours and serve with whipped cream.

—Mary McCarty

GINGERBREAD WAFFLES

Topped with scoops of vanilla ice cream, these make a big hit.

Yield: 10-12

1 cup dark molasses
½ cup milk
1 egg yolk, slightly beaten
2 cups flour
1 tsp. salt
1¼ tsp. baking soda
2½ tsp. ginger
1¼ tsp. cinnamon
¼ tsp. cloves
⅓ cup cooking oil
1 egg white, stiffly beaten

Combine molasses, milk, and egg yolk. Add dry ingredients, then oil. Mix well. Fold in egg white. Cook in hot waffle iron.

—Debbie Heishman, Chambersburg, Pennsylvania

"Submit yourselves therefore to God. Resist the devil, and he will flee from you" (James 4:7). The Lord has been dealing with me about losing pounds for His glory. Success was up and down. As I read this verse, the Lord seemed to speak to my heart, "You know you are in My will losing pounds. The next time the devil tempts you to eat something you shouldn't, or to overeat, tell him your will is submitted to God and to take the matter up with Him." Much to my amazement, when I tried this the gnawing stomach cravings disappeared almost immediately.

—Linda Johnson, Turner, Montana

DESSERTS

FLAN

This is a popular Mexican custard.

Oven: 350°   Serves: 4-6

2 cups milk
½ cup sugar
1 stick cinnamon
4 eggs
1 tsp. vanilla
¼ cup sugar

Scald milk with ½ cup sugar and cinnamon. Beat eggs with vanilla. Pour milk mixture over eggs, stirring quickly. Melt (caramelize) ¼ cup sugar over medium heat and pour on bottom of baking dish. Pour custard over sugar. Place in another pan with hot water about 1" deep. Bake until table knife comes out clean and custard is set.

—Margo Sterling, Churubusco, Mexico

WHAT TO DO WITH YOUR BIBLE:
1. Study it through (Josh. 1:8).
2. Pray it in (Ps. 119:18).
3. Put it down (Ps. 119:103).
4. Work it out (Ps. 119:15).
5. Pass it on to others (Ps. 119:27, 46).

RHUBARB SAUCE

May be eaten as is, or as a topping for ice cream.

2 qts. rhubarb, chopped
sugar, to taste
1 pkg. (3 oz.) strawberry gelatin

Cook rhubarb, sweeten, remove from heat, and stir in gelatin powder.

—Betty Steiro, New Westminster, B.C., Canada

Hardened brown sugar can be restored to its original moist condition by freezing it. When thawed, it is soft again.

—Priscilla Bennett, Pacifica, California

"What dainty morsels rumors are. They are eaten with great relish!" (Prov. 18:8 TLB).

One way of reducing the number of squabbles among your children is to print an appropriate Scripture verse in large letters on cardboard, and hang it on the wall when they get into a fight. Keep it there until all the children have memorized it. You can check on their memorization at meal times. Some verses you might use are: Psalms 34:14; 94:7-11; 133:1; Proverbs 12:20; 16:7; 20:3; Zechariah 8:19; Matthew 5:9; 10:28; Mark 9:50; John 14:27; Romans 8:35; 12:18; 14:19; Galatians 5:22; Ephesians 4:3; Colossians 3:15; 2 Timothy 2:22; Hebrews 12:14; 1 Peter 3:14-16. One of the modern translations may be easier to understand than the King James Version.

—LaVerne Johnson, Portland, Oregon

To help young children memorize Bible verses, make a chart. List the verses down the left side in alphabetical order. For example: "All we like sheep have gone astray," "Believe on the Lord Jesus Christ," "Children, obey your parents," "Draw nigh to God," etc. List the days of the week across the top of the chart, and include an extra space after the last day. Then draw lines, forming squares.

Each evening, if the children can say their verse perfectly, they put a star in that day's space. At the end of the week, they put a "Jesus" sticker in the extra space if they have stars for every day.

At the end of twenty-six weeks, give them a reward for work well done.

—Mrs. Glen Snader, Mount Joy, Pennsylvania

"Teach a child to choose the right path, and when he is older he will remain upon it" (Prov. 22:6).

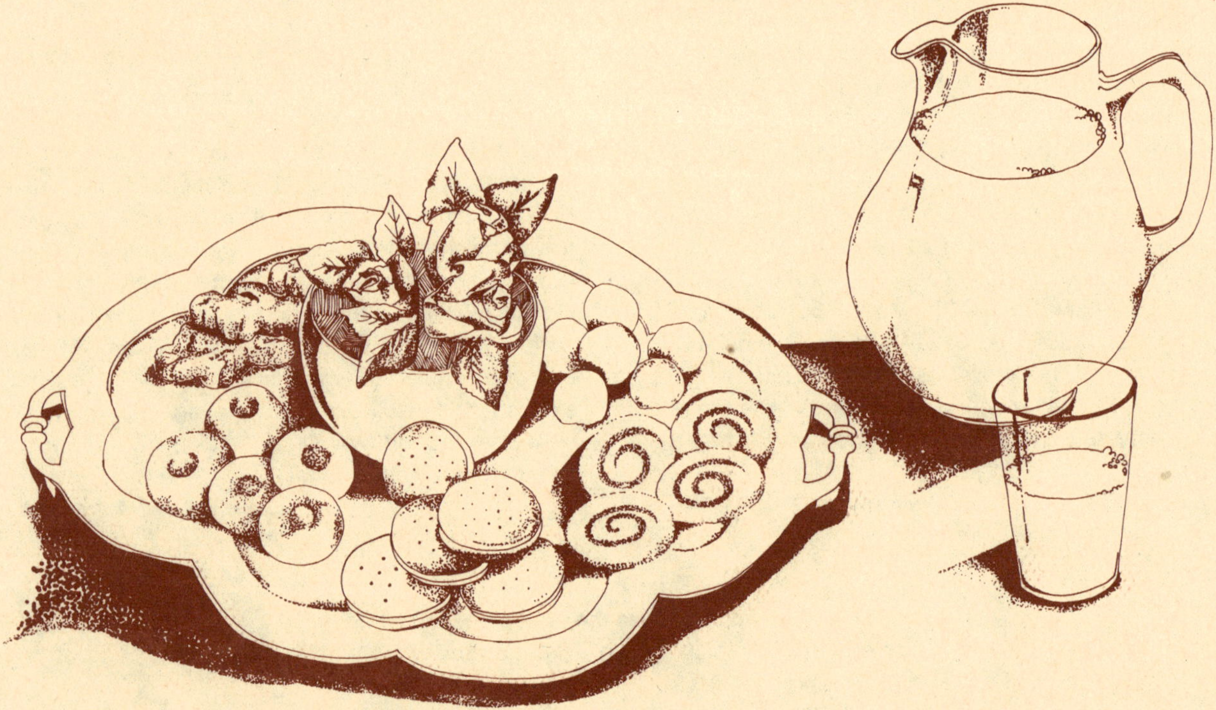

Cakes, Cookies and Snacks

A group of Philippine women were sitting on the floor looking at *National Geographic* magazines. Suddenly, they began giggling.

"What's so funny?" their hostess asked.

"Oh, look!" They pointed to a picture of a street scene in an ordinary American city, with people walking down a sidewalk. They started to laugh again. "The people are so *fat*!"

Have you ever thought about what we might look like to people in other parts of the world, especially to slender Asians? Probably no other people are so conscious of weight and diets than we; but probably no other people have such an excess of fattening foods available.

We, as Christian women, should be disciplined enough to stop before we open the refrigerator door for another snack, to resist reaching for another cookie.

"Discipline," says Richard S. Taylor, "is the ability to regulate conduct by principle and judgment rather than impulse, desire, high pressure, or social custom."

The Lord can help us to discipline our eating.

APPLE PUDDING CAKE

That special man in your life will thank you when you serve him this cake.

Oven: 350°

5 Tbsp. soft margarine
1 cup sugar
1 egg, beaten
3 cups apples, diced
½ cup walnuts, chopped
1 tsp. vanilla
1 cup flour, sifted
1 tsp. soda
½ tsp. salt
¼ tsp. nutmeg
½ tsp. cinnamon

Cream margarine and sugar, add egg and mix well. Stir in apples, walnuts, and vanilla. Sift flour with soda, salt, nutmeg, and cinnamon. Stir in dry ingredients, just until there are no traces of flour. Pour into greased 8" square pan and bake 40 to 45 minutes.

—Romaine Bryner, Washington, Pennsylvania

APPLE CAKE

A nourishing and tasty cake.

Oven: 350°

2 eggs, beaten
1 cup honey
½ cup cooking oil
2 cups flour, sifted
2 tsp. baking powder
½ tsp. soda
½ tsp. salt
1 tsp. cinnamon
½ cup rolled oats
4 cups grated apples
1 cup raisins
½ cup nuts

   Beat eggs slightly. Add honey and oil. Sift together flour, baking powder, soda, salt, and cinnamon and add to liquid mixture. Fold in oats, apples, raisins, and nuts. Pour into greased, floured, 9"x13" pan. Bake for 45 minutes. Serve with whipped cream or ice cream, if desired.

—Vi Dormier, Bothell, Washington

APPLESAUCE CAKE

Try substituting one-half cup whole wheat flour for the same amount of white flour. Whole wheat provides lots of minerals, vitamins, and protein for you and your family.

Oven: 350°

2½ cups flour
1½ cups sugar
¼ tsp. baking powder
1½ tsp. soda
1½ tsp. salt
¾ tsp. cinnamon
½ tsp. cloves
½ tsp. allspice
½ cup shortening
½ cup water
2 eggs
1½ cups applesauce
½ cup chopped walnuts

   Mix dry ingredients. Add shortening, water, and applesauce. Beat. Add eggs. Beat. Stir in walnuts. Bake 35-40 minutes for layers, or 45-50 minutes for 9"x13" pan.

—Sandy Parrott, Moline, Illinois

RASPBERRY YOGURT CAKE

Just right to serve Auntie when she comes for tea. It's not too sweet, but very tasty.

Oven: 350°

½ cup butter
1 cup brown or white sugar
1 egg
1 tsp. vanilla
2 cups flour
1 tsp. soda
½ tsp. baking powder
¼ tsp. salt
1 carton (8 oz.) raspberry yogurt

Cream butter and sugar. Add egg and vanilla; beat until light. Sift dry ingredients and add to creamed mixture alternately with yogurt, mixing well. Pour into buttered 9" tube pan. Bake 25 minutes or until done. Let stand 10 minutes before removing from pan. You may also use peach, cherry, or blueberry yogurt instead of raspberry.

—Nickalene Johnson, Poulsbo, Washington

There never was a feast without a sacrifice.

CARROT PINEAPPLE CAKE

A moist cake set off by the tangy taste of cream cheese frosting.

Oven: 350°

1¾ cups flour
1 tsp. baking powder
1½ tsp. soda
1 tsp. cinnamon
½ tsp. salt
⅔ cup salad oil
1 cup honey
2 eggs
1 cup carrot, finely shredded
½ cup crushed pineapple, with syrup
1 tsp. vanilla

Sift dry ingredients together into large mixing bowl. Add rest of ingredients and mix until moistened and then beat 2 minutes at medium speed. Bake in greased and lightly floured 9" square pan 50 minutes or until done. Cover with foil while baking if top gets too brown. Cool and frost.

CREAM CHEESE FROSTING

2 pkgs. (3 oz.) cream cheese, softened
1 Tbsp. butter, softened
1 tsp. vanilla
1¾ cups powdered sugar, sifted

Mix in bowl and beat with electric mixer. If necessary, add milk to make of spreading consistency.

—Marcene McFarland, Kirkland, Washington

"Teach the older women to be quiet and respectful in everything they do. They must not go around speaking evil of others and must not be heavy drinkers, but they should be teachers of goodness. These older women must train the younger women to live quietly, to love their husbands and their children, and to be sensible and clean minded, spending their time in their own homes, being kind and obedient to their husbands, so that the Christian faith can't be spoken against by those who know them" (Titus 2:3-5 TLB).

EGGLESS HILLBILLY CAKE

This recipe is easy enough to be made by the younger members of your family.

Oven: 350°

1 cup sugar
1 cup water
1 tsp. cinnamon
½ tsp. salt
1 tsp. allspice
½ cup butter
1 cup raisins
2 cups flour
2 tsp. soda
1 tsp. baking powder

　Combine everything *except* flour, soda, and baking powder. Boil 1 minute. Blend in flour, soda, and baking powder. Pour into greased loaf pan. Bake 30 minutes or until done. Spread topping over warm cake and place under broiler until bubbly. Serve warm or cold.

Topping:
⅔ cup brown sugar
¼ cup butter
3 Tbsp. milk
½ cup coconut
½ cup raisins
½ cup nuts, chopped or ¾ cup rolled oats

　Melt butter with brown sugar. Add rest of ingredients and spread over cake.

—Marlene Ratzlaff, Wasilla, Alaska

BANANA CAKE

We should thank the Lord that bananas are available to us all year, everywhere.

Oven: 350°　　Serves: 15

2 cups flour
2 eggs, beaten
1 cup bananas, mashed
1½ cups sugar
½ cup shortening
¼ tsp. salt
1 tsp. vanilla
½ cup buttermilk
1 tsp. baking soda

　Cream sugar and shortening. Add salt, vanilla, and eggs. Beat well. Add bananas and buttermilk alternately. Sift flour and soda, mix with rest. Pour in greased, lightly floured, 9" x 13" pan. Bake for 30-35 minutes.

—Bobbie Baker, Carrollton, Michigan

SHOEFLY CAKE

Simple to make and easy to eat!

Oven: 350°

4 cups flour
2 cups brown sugar
¾ cup shortening
1 cup molasses
1 Tbsp. soda
2 cups boiling water

Mix flour, brown sugar, and shortening together. Save 1 cup of crumbs for top of cake. Add molasses, soda, and boiling water to rest of crumbs and pour into 9" x 12" pan. Sprinkle reserved crumbs on top and bake 45-50 minutes.

—Mary Shank, Mechanicsburg, Pennsylvania

"Don't worry about anything; instead, pray about everything; tell God your needs and don't forget to thank him for his answers. If you do this you will experience God's peace, which is far more wonderful than the human mind can understand. His peace will keep your thoughts and your hearts quiet and at rest as you trust in Christ Jesus" (Phil. 4:6-7 TLB).

POPPY SEED CAKE

As a dessert, this cake is usually a winner with men. Sift confectioner's sugar over each slice.

Oven: 350°

¾ cup poppy seeds
⅓ cup honey
¼ cup water
2½ cups flour, sifted
1 tsp. soda
1 tsp. salt
1 cup butter
1½ cups sugar
4 eggs, separated
1 cup sour cream
1 tsp. vanilla

Combine poppy seeds, honey, and water in saucepan and cook over medium heat for 5 minutes. Cool. Sift dry ingredients and set aside. Cream butter and sugar. Add poppy seed mix, then egg yolks, beating well. Add dry ingredients alternately with sour cream and vanilla. Fold in stiffly-beaten egg whites. After egg whites have been evenly folded into mixture, pour into 2 loaf pans that have been generously greased and lightly floured. Bake 1 hour and 15 minutes. Cool 10 minutes and turn out on wire rack.

—Naomi Homme, Anchorage, Alaska

OATMEAL CAKE

A moist cake but keeps well — if it isn't eaten up right away!

Oven: 350°

- 1 cup rolled oats
- 1 cup raisins
- 1¼ cups boiling water
- 1 cup brown sugar
- ½ cup margarine
- 1 tsp. vanilla
- 2 eggs
- 1½ cups flour
- 1 tsp. soda
- 1 tsp. cinnamon
- ½ tsp. salt
- ½ tsp. nutmeg

Pour water over oats and raisins. Cover and set aside. Cream brown sugar, margarine, and vanilla. Add eggs, then the oats; mix well. Stir in dry ingredients and mix well. Bake in 9" x 13" pan for 35 minutes.

—Ann Thomas, Seattle, Washington

FRUIT SURPRISE CAKE

A wonderful moist cake dotted with fruits.

Oven: 325°

- 2 cups flour
- 1½ cups sugar
- 1 tsp. salt
- 2 tsp. baking soda
- 1 can (1 lb.) fruit cocktail, undrained
- 2 eggs
- 2 tsp. vanilla
- ½ cup brown sugar
- ½ cup nuts, chopped

Mix everything together except nuts and brown sugar. Pour into 9" x 13" pan. Make topping by mixing brown sugar with nuts. Sprinkle over top of batter. Bake 45 minutes.

—Anna Mary Weaver, New Holland, Pennsylvania

SNAPPY CAKE

You can make this cake even when you have run out of eggs.

Oven: 350°

1 cup brown sugar
1½ cups water
1 cup raisins
2 oz. citron, cut fine
⅓ cup shortening
1 tsp. cinnamon
¼ tsp. cloves
¼ tsp. nutmeg
½ tsp. salt
2 cups flour
5 tsp. baking powder
½ tsp. vanilla

    Boil sugar, water, raisins, citron, shortening, spices, and salt together for 3 minutes. Let cool. Add flour, baking powder, and vanilla. Mix well. Turn into greased loaf pan. Bake 45 minutes.

—Patricia McCash, Frankfort, Michigan

My life
has grown in love,
with pain,
tears,
and smiling face —
just today.

—Diane Walsh, Delanson, New York

POUND CAKE

This cake doesn't need frosting. Slice it, toast it, and serve with crushed fresh strawberries.

Oven: 325º

1 cup margarine
3 cups sugar
½ cup oil
6 eggs
1 Tbsp. vanilla
3⅔ cups flour
½ tsp. salt
½ tsp. baking powder
1 cup milk

    Cream together margarine, sugar, oil, and eggs. Add vanilla. Sift flour, salt, and baking powder together and add alternately with milk. Beat well after each addition. Pour into greased 10" tube pan. Bake for 1 hour, 25 minutes. Let cool in pan for 20 minutes. Run knife around edge of pan while hot. Turn out onto plate.

—Mary Therrien, Lansing, Michigan

"Let us consider how to stimulate one another to love and good deeds" (Heb. 10:24 NASB).

GRAHAM CRACKER CAKE

This cake is good with a vanilla custard between the layers and frosted with chocolate frosting.

Oven: 350º

3 cups graham cracker crumbs
1 Tbsp. baking powder
¼ tsp. salt
3 eggs, separated
1½ cups milk
¾ cup shortening
1½ cups sugar
1 tsp. vanilla

    Grease and flour two 9" pans.
    Combine crumbs, baking powder, and salt. Beat together egg yolks, milk, shortening, sugar, and vanilla until smooth. Add to cracker crumbs; mix well. Beat egg whites until stiff, and fold in. Pour into pans and bake 30-35 minutes. Cool 5 minutes in pans before turning out onto a rack.

—Lois Beard, Sherwood, Oregon

SCRIPTURE CAKE

Read Luke 14:15, the last part.

Oven: 325°

¾ cup Psalms 55:21a (½ cup shortening, ¼ cup oil)
1 cup Jeremiah 6:20 (sugar)
3 of Isaiah 10:14 (eggs)
2¼ cups 1 Kings 4:22a (flour)
1 tsp. 1 Corinthians 5:6 (baking powder)
Pinch of Matthew 5:13 (salt)
¼ cup Judges 4:19b (milk)
1 Tbsp. Judges 14:18 (honey)
¼ tsp. 2 Chronicles 9:9 (nutmeg)
1 tsp. 2 Chronicles 9:9 (allspice)
2 tsp. 2 Chronicles 9:9 (cinnamon)
1 tsp. 2 Chronicles 9:9 (cloves)
1 cup 2 Samuel 16:1b (raisins)
1 cup Song of Solomon 2:13a (figs or dates)
1 cup Numbers 17:8 (almonds), chopped

    Cream shortening, oil, and sugar together, then add eggs one at a time. Proverbs 23:14 (beat) well. Sift and measure flour, baking powder, and salt. Add alternately to sugar mixture with milk. Stir in honey and spices, then raisins, figs (or dates), and almonds. 2 Kings 4:5 (pour) into well-greased vessels (loaf pans or a 9"x13" pan) and Leviticus 24:5 (bake) for 45 minutes. Cool in pan. After a few John 11:9 (hours), slice and Proverbs 23:1 (eat).

—Nancy Kallinen, Bothell, Washington

LUSCIOUS FROSTING

This is enough icing to frost a 2-layer cake very generously. It stays soft for days!

1 cup milk
¼ cup flour
1 cup butter
1 cup sugar
2 tsp. vanilla

    Combine flour and milk until smooth. Cook and stir in saucepan over medium heat until thick. Remove from heat and cool thoroughly. Cream butter and sugar until light and fluffy. Add the cold flour and milk mixture with vanilla and beat briskly until the mixture is light and fluffy and sugar crystals have disappeared.

—Eileen Zimmerman, Kelso, Washington

"Are you so foolish? Having begun by the Spirit, are you now being perfected by the flesh?" (Gal. 3:3 NASB).

GINGERBREAD

An old favorite with a new, healthful twist.

Oven: 375°

1½ cups fine whole wheat flour
1 tsp. baking soda
½ tsp. salt
½ tsp. ginger
1 tsp. cinnamon
¼ cup vegetable oil
¼ cup maple syrup
¼ cup honey
½ carton (8 oz.) yogurt
1 egg

Combine the dry ingredients in a large bowl and mix well with a fork. Combine the liquid ingredients, mixing together, then add to dry ingredients. Beat until smooth.

Pour into a greased 8" square pan. Bake 30-35 minutes, or until done. Let cool in pan, and cut.

—Mary Wren, San Jose, California

CARROT COOKIES

Experiment by adding a little bit of wheat germ to a cookie recipe. It helps maintain health.

Oven: 400°

1 cup sugar
1 egg
½ cup grated carrots
2 cups sifted flour
½ cup butter
1 tsp. lemon flavoring
½ cup raisins, chopped
2 tsp. baking powder
½ tsp. salt

Mix and drop by teaspoonfuls on cookie sheet. Bake for 10-12 minutes.

—Helen Dale, Beeton, Ontario, Canada

Try cutting down on the amount of sugar called for in cookie and cake recipes. Depending on the recipe, you may cut the amount of sugar by ¼, ⅓, or even ½. This does not usually alter the quality of the product and is more healthful for your family.

—Linda Johnson, Turner, Montana

GRANDMA'S OATMEAL COOKIES

Do not refrigerate this dough to bake at a later time. Bake it all at once.

Oven: 350°   Yield: 12-16 dozen

2 cups sugar
2 cups flour
6 cups rolled oats
1 tsp. salt
1 lb. margarine, softened
2 tsp. baking soda
½ cup boiling water

    Mix sugar, flour, oats, and salt. Add margarine and mix well. Dissolve soda in boiling water and add. Mix well. Drop by teaspoonfuls on cookie sheet. Flatten with a fork. Bake 12-15 minutes.

—Blanche Van Tol, Surrey, B.C., Canada

SOFT SUGAR COOKIES

Dress them up with a sprinkle of red or green sugar on top, before baking.

Oven: 375°

4 eggs
2 cups sugar
1 cup brown sugar
1 cup shortening
pinch of salt
½ cup margarine
1½ cups buttermilk or sour milk
1½ tsp. baking soda
3 cups flour
3 tsp. baking powder
2 cups flour
1 Tbsp. vanilla

    Cream together eggs, sugars, salt, shortening, and margarine. Mix together the buttermilk and soda, and add to the shortening mixture. Add the 3 cups flour and the baking powder and mix well. Add the remaining flour and vanilla. Drop by teaspoonfuls onto baking sheet. Bake 7-10 minutes.

—Edith Groff, Manheim, Pennsylvania

"Pleasant words are a honeycomb, sweet to the soul, and healing to the bones" (Prov. 16:24 NASB).

HONEY SPICE SNAPS

Ivene says that these are her grandson's favorite.

Oven: 350°

2¼ cups flour
½ tsp. salt
½ tsp. cinnamon
1½ tsp soda
1 tsp. ginger
¼ tsp. cloves
1 cup brown sugar
¼ cup honey
¾ cup shortening
1 egg

Sift flour, salt, cinnamon, soda, ginger, and cloves together. Set aside. Cream shortening and brown sugar well. Blend in unbeaten egg and honey. Add dry ingredients gradually and mix well. Chill dough. Shape into balls and dip into sugar to glaze. Place sugared side up on ungreased baking sheet. Bake 12 to 15 minutes.

—Ivene Goemaere, Bothell, Washington

MIGHTY GOOD DROP COOKIES

Wheat germ will boost your family's health.

Oven: 350°   Yield: 3 dozen

½ cup shortening
1 cup brown sugar
¼ cup milk
2 eggs
2¼ cups whole wheat flour
2 tsp. baking powder
½ cup wheat germ
2 tsp. nutmeg

Cream shortening and add sugar gradually. Add milk and beaten eggs, then stir in dry ingredients. Beat well. Drop by teaspoonfuls on greased sheet. Bake for 8 minutes.

—Helen Hitchin, Walnut Creek, California

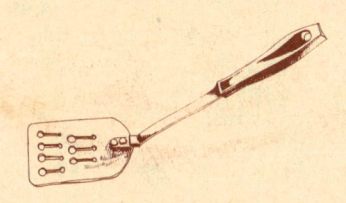

APPLE BARS

Cut in small bars to serve as cookies or larger squares to serve with ice cream as dessert.

Oven: 350°

½ cup soft shortening
¾ cup honey (or 1 cup sugar)
1 egg
1½ cups whole wheat flour
½ tsp. salt
1½ tsp. soda
2½ cups grated, peeled apples
   (use medium grater, pack lightly)
1 cup brown sugar
1 tsp. cinnamon
1 cup walnuts, chopped

Grease and flour a 15" x 10" x 1" jelly roll pan. Beat shortening, sugar, and egg together until fluffy. Combine whole wheat flour, salt, and soda in a small bowl and mix with a fork until blended. Add to the shortening mixture and stir well (mixture will be stiff). Add apples and blend well. Spread evenly in prepared pan. Mix brown sugar, cinnamon, and nuts and sprinkle evenly over batter.

Bake about 30 minutes or until set in the middle. Cool in pan.

—Elsie E. White, Surrey, B.C., Canada

We Shall Never Be Sorry For —

Doing good to all,
Speaking evil of no one,
Hearing all sides before deciding,
Thinking before speaking,
Holding an angry tongue,
Asking forgiveness for all wrongs,
Being patient towards all,
Disbelieving evil reports.

— Submitted by Gloria Zip, Saskatoon, Saskatchewan

Honey Substitution:

In most recipes, replace one cup of sugar or corn syrup with one-half cup honey.

If a recipe calls for additional liquid, omit ¼ cup for each cup of honey used.

When using honey in cookies or cakes, add ½ tsp. soda for every cup of honey used. Bake at a lower temperature.

CAROB BROWNIES

Carob is a cocoa substitute. It may be purchased at health food stores.

Oven: 300°

3/4 cup oil
1 cup brown sugar
4 eggs
1 cup whole wheat flour
3/4 cup carob powder
few grains salt
1 cup walnuts, chopped
2 tsp. vanilla

    Beat together oil, sugar, and eggs. Add carob powder with other dry ingredients and mix thoroughly. Add nuts and vanilla. Spread in greased and floured 9" x 13" pan. Bake 25-30 minutes. Cool and cut into squares.

                —Karis Taylor, Mountlake Terrace, Washington

PUMPKIN BARS

Wonderful for a coffee-break or dessert.

Oven: 350°

2 cups flour
2 tsp. baking powder
1/2 tsp. salt
2 tsp. cinnamon
1 tsp. soda
2 cups sugar
1 cup oil
4 eggs, beaten slightly
2 cups pumpkin

    Combine in bowl in order given. Beat well. Spread on greased jelly roll pan (12" x 15"). Bake 25 minutes. Cool. Frost with cream cheese frosting (see page 132).

                —Ruth Tervol, Milton, Washington

COOKIES

OATMEAL COOKIE BARS

Especially good for lunch boxes!

Oven: 325°

1 cup oil
2 cups brown sugar
1 cup granulated sugar
1 cup water
2 tsp. vanilla
2 cups flour
1½ tsp. salt
1 tsp. soda
1 tsp. baking powder
6 cups quick oats

Combine oil, sugars, water, and vanilla. Beat well. Add flour, salt, soda, baking powder to first mixture, blending well. Stir in oats. Spread into well-greased 9" x 13" pan. Bake 15-20 minutes. Do not overbake.

I like to add: 2 tsp. cinnamon and ½ tsp. nutmeg with the flour, and 1-2 cups raisins with the oats.

—Marlene Ratzlaff, Wasilla, Alaska

"Do not be carried away by varied and strange teachings; for it is good for the heart to be strengthened by grace..." (Heb. 13:9 NASB).

FIVE STEPS TO VICTORY
1. Fret not
2. Trust in the Lord
3. Delight in the Lord
4. Commit your way to the Lord
5. Rest in the Lord

(Psa. 37:1-7)

AUSTRIAN PILLOWS

These little pastries delight the eye and the tongue. Read 1 Corinthians 10:31 to keep your perspective.

Oven: 375°

3 oz. cream cheese
½ cup margarine
1 cup flour
jam

Cut the cheese and margarine into small pieces. Mix in the flour until smooth and place in refrigerator for 2 hours. Roll out into one thin piece, cut into squares. Put small dot of jam (preferably black raspberry) in the center of each piece. Fold over dough to form triangles or rectangles. Pinch pillow together so jam won't run out. Cut few slits in top of pillows. Bake 10-12 minutes.

—Alberta W. Mechley, Cincinnati, Ohio

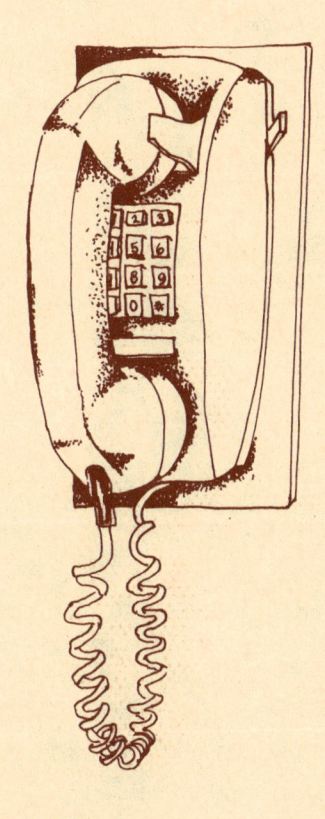

TELEPHONE BARS

The friend who gave me this recipe said that every time she served it, her guests telephoned the next day for the recipe!

Oven: 350°

1 cup chopped dates
1 tsp. soda
1 cup boiling water
½ cup shortening
1 cup sugar
2 eggs
1 tsp. vanilla
¼ tsp. salt
2 Tbsp. cocoa
1½ cups flour
1 cup chocolate chips, if desired

Pour the boiling water over the chopped dates and soda in a small bowl. Mix and cool. Cream the sugar and shortening. Add the eggs, vanilla, salt, and cocoa. Then add the flour alternately with the date mixture and beat well. Spread in a greased 9" x 13" pan and sprinkle chocolate chips on top. You may substitute ½ cup of whole wheat flour for ½ cup of the white flour. Bake 30 to 35 minutes.

—Peggy Page, River Falls, Wisconsin

CASSEROLE COOKIES

An unusual method that gives fine results. These are good for "special" occasions.

Oven: 350°   Yield: 2 dozen

2 eggs
1 cup sugar
1 cup chopped dates
1 cup flaked coconut
1 cup chopped walnuts
1 tsp. vanilla
¼ tsp. almond flavoring

   Beat eggs in a buttered casserole. Add sugar. Mix in remaining ingredients. Bake in an uncovered casserole for 35 minutes. Stir several times while baking. Remove from oven, let cool, oil your hands, and form into balls. Roll in powdered sugar.

—Emily Taylor, Juneau, Alaska

   Pure lemon extract will remove the ink-stamped price mark on products.

— Nancy Smith, Dublin, Georgia

DATE DROPS

Tiny sweets for your sweetheart.

1 lb. dates, cut up
¾ cup sugar
1 tsp. vanilla
¾ tsp. salt
½ cup margarine
4 cups Rice Krispies

   Cook dates, sugar, vanilla, salt, and margarine over low heat, stirring constantly. Let cool, then add Rice Krispies.

   Form this mixture into balls, and roll in finely chopped nuts and/or coconut.

—Betty Brooks, Rapid City, Illinois

"The precepts of the Lord are right, rejoicing the heart; the commandment of the Lord is pure, enlightening the eyes . . . They are more desirable than gold, yes, than much fine gold; sweeter also than honey and the drippings of the honeycomb" (Ps. 19:8, 10 NASB).

HOLIDAY COOKIE RECIPE

by Busy Mother

Take 1 cup butter. Find Tom's shoes. Melt butter, tie Tom's shoes. Spread peanut butter on 3 slices bread for three small children. Rescue overbrown butter from stove. Add 1½ cups sugar to butter. Get 2 eggs and some milk from refrigerator. Pour 3 glasses of milk to rinse down peanut butter. Wipe up first spilled glass. Mop up egg, which rolled off counter and get another egg from refrigerator and add to butter and sugar.

Get small children interested in coloring and then spell words for first grader. Sift 2½ cups flour with 1 tsp. baking powder, 1 tsp. soda, and ½ tsp. salt. Measure 1 cup oatmeal. Take marble out of baby's mouth. Ask someone if you added 1 or 2 cups oatmeal to batter.

Screaming may help at this point, but it's time-consuming. Find recipe in pile of drawings and continue. Measure 1 cup cornflakes and 1 cup coconut. Big children want to know if cookies are baked yet. The dog, Moose, is in the way, so remove to outside. Put batter in refrigerator to chill. Peel 3 oranges for children. Mop up counter, table, floor, and cupboard doors. Moose is let in. Remove batter and Moose's nose from refrigerator. Wash hands, drop cookies on pan, and place in hot oven. Allow children to help drop cookies and forget the blobs on the floor. Moose will take care of them. Repeat procedure until all are baked. At this point, mop up table, floor, and counter.

Be sure to have a holiday spirit. Smile. Make mental note to start cookies after children are in bed next year.

—Barbara DeLamater, Hillsdale, New York

BUTTER KRISPS

You will have to hide these buttery delights if you want to serve them for dinner.

Oven: 350°

½ lb. graham crackers
slivered almonds
½ cup butter
½ cup margarine
½ cup sugar

Lay graham crackers in jelly roll pans right together. Spread almonds over them. Boil butter, margarine, and sugar together for 2 minutes and pour over the crackers and bake for 10-12 minutes. Remove from pan.

—Alsea Britton, Lewis, Kansas

COOKIES WHILE YOU SLEEP

Fun to make with the "help" of small children.

Oven: 350°   Yield: 5 dozen or more

2 egg whites
pinch of salt
¼ tsp. cream of tartar
⅔ cup sugar
1 tsp. vanilla
¼ tsp. almond flavoring
1 cup pecans, chopped
¾ cup chocolate chips

Beat egg whites until foamy; add salt and cream of tartar and continue to beat until stiff. Gradually add sugar, vanilla, and almond flavoring. Peaks should be shiny and stiff. Fold in pecans and chips. Drop by teaspoon on greased cookie sheet. Place in pre-heated oven, turn off heat and leave oven closed until morning. Don't peek. You may add food coloring for more colorful cookies.

—Mrs. Jim Betts, Salina, Kansas

Put wax paper over the ends of the curtain rods so that your curtains will slip onto the rods easily.

—Evelyn Daniel, Sonora, California

Forgiveness is like the fragrance of a flower shed on the heel that crushed it.

—Gladys Gage, Point Gibson, Missouri

TRAIL LOGS

Lynn and her family do lots of hiking and find these "logs" are high in energy. Good for school snacks, too.

Yield: 2½ dozen

¼ cup dry roasted cashews
1¼ cups walnuts
6 dried black figs
½ cup dates, pitted
¼ cup dried apples
¼ cup seedless raisins
¼ tsp. lemon juice
1 Tbsp. apple cider
2 Tbsp. powdered sugar *or* **½ cup flaked coconut**

Run nuts and fruit through the fine blade of a food chopper and mix thoroughly. Blend in lemon juice and cider. Using about a tablespoon at a time, roll the mixture into small logs each about 2" by ¾". Roll the logs in powdered sugar or coconut and allow to stand uncovered for a day or two to dry. Store in refrigerator or wrap tightly in foil or plastic film to carry on the trail.

—Lynn Bacon, Anchorage, Alaska

LOW-CAL DANISH

Breakfast, lunch, or snack — this goodie fits in anywhere.

1 slice lightly toasted bread (unbuttered)
¼ cup cottage cheese
1 heaping Tbsp. applesauce

Spread cottage cheese on toast and add applesauce. Sprinkle with cinnamon or nutmeg. Place under broiler for a few minutes until cheese is heated and begins to bubble. Serve immediately.

Variations: fresh strawberries or peaches, lightly sweetened. For these fruits omit cinnamon and nutmeg. Add fruits last — after cheese is heated through. These variations make an excellent dessert.

—JoAnn McMoran, Edmonds, Washington

"The kingdom of heaven is like a treasure hidden in the field, which a man found and hid; and from joy over it he goes and sells all that he has, and buys that field" (Matt. 13:44 NASB).

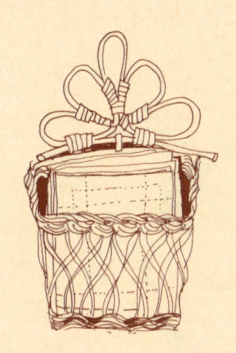

CAROB KISSES

The combination of peanut butter, milk powder, and sesame seeds give plenty of protein to active youngsters.

¼ cup honey
½ cup peanut butter
½ cup nuts, chopped
½ cup coconut
¼ cup carob powder
¼ cup dry powdered milk

Mix and knead. Roll into small balls. Pinch top to form a "kiss" and chill. May add raisins or sesame seeds.

—Carolyn Rasmussen, Bellevue, Washington

GRANOLA

Cereal? Snack? Granola is so good that it can be eaten any time.

Oven: 250°

¾ cup oil
¾ cup honey
1½ Tbsp. vanilla
⅓ cup water
½ Tbsp. salt
8 cups rolled oats (quick)
1 cup wheat germ
1 cup coconut
¼ cup brown sugar
1 cup nuts (combination of chopped peanuts, almonds, sunflower seeds, sesame seeds, etc.)

Whip together oil, honey, vanilla, water, and salt until well mixed. Pour this over the remaining ingredients and mix well. Spread ½" deep in shallow baking pans. Bake for 30 minutes. Stir. Continue baking, stirring every 15 minutes, until golden brown — about 1½ hours.

—Julie Wayner, Edmonds, Washington

HOMEMADE POPSICLES

Summertime favorites!

ORANGE SASSY
1 env. plain gelatin
½ cup cold water
2½ cups boiling water
2 Tbsp. sugar
1 cup concentrated orange juice

In a quart measuring cup, sprinkle gelatin over cold water and let stand 5 minutes until soft. Add boiling water and stir briefly until gelatin is completely dissolved. Mix in sugar and then orange juice. Fill molds, ice trays, muffin tins, or cups and freeze about 6 hours or until solid.

PURPLE COW
1 envelope plain gelatin
⅔ cup cold water
2⅔ cup reconstituted dry milk
⅔ cup grape juice concentrate

In small saucepan, sprinkle gelatin over cold water and let stand 5 minutes until soft. Cook over low heat about 1 minute until gelatin is dissolved. Add milk and stir in grape juice. Fill molds and freeze.

—Sandi Gotsch, Oakland, Missouri

FANTASTIC NUTS & BOLTS

A great snack for any occasion, having fewer calories and more nutrition than sweet snacks. It may be kept several months by storing in air-tight containers.

Oven: 250°   Serves: 50

1 pkg. Cheerios
1 pkg. Rice Chex
1 pkg. Wheat Chex
1 pkg. Corn Chex
1 or 2 pkg. Pretzel Stix
2 or 3 cans of mixed nuts
1 lb. margarine
1 Tbsp. Beau Monde seasoning
¾ Tbsp. smoke-flavored salt
1½ tsp. marjoram
1½ tsp. summer savory
½ tsp. garlic powder
1 tsp. onion powder
⅛ tsp. cayenne pepper

Mix cereals, pretzels, and nuts carefully in one large roasting pan or two other pans. Pulverize the marjoram and summer savory and blend with other seasonings. Blend with cereals. Cut margarine in small pieces and dot over entire surface. Cook for one hour, stirring several times.

—Katie Fortune, Edmonds, Washington

Got a Minute?

She mended a doll
And the washing waited.
The dust lay
While the fish hook was baited.

When "injuns" attacked,
Her dinner burned up.
She provided a bed
For a straying pup.

A two-year-old helped
With the cookie dough.
The ironing dried out
While she romped in the snow.

Her neighbors whispered
To one another;
But the children laughed
And adored their mother.

—Submitted by Linda Kilburn, Taylor, Michigan

SNACKS FOR CHILDREN

Children use up lots of energy. Often after school or after playing hard, they need something for a snack. It can be a problem finding snacks that are good for them yet are appealing. Be sure to tell the children that healthful snacks will help them have clear skin, shiny hair, and more strength.

Here are some ideas for snacks that are nutritious, good, and easily made:

1. On the counter, in separate jars, put sunflower seeds, raisins and almonds mixed, dried prunes or figs, peanuts or soy nuts.
2. Instead of pop or kool-aid, use fresh fruit juices or unsweetened canned and bottled juices.
3. Hard boiled eggs. Make them pink once in a while, if you have any beet juice!
4. A variety of cheeses, eaten with whole wheat crackers or bread. A slice of cheese on a piece of whole wheat bread sprinkled with wheat germ and toasted will fill up any hungry boy.
5. Carrots and celery and radishes are good and crunchy.
6. Fresh fruit.

Do not keep candy, ice cream, pop, potato chips, and cookies around.

At first, the children may eat great quantities of these snacks, and you will be alarmed at the cost. But you can be sure that after a short time, the rate of consumption will slow down. The human body can be starved for the vitamins and minerals that natural foods supply. When this need is filled, the body will not demand as much of the natural foods as it did the over-refined kind.

As you make these healthful snacks available to your children, you will know that you are cooperating with the Lord in maintaining their good health.

ZIP, ZEST, AND ZING

Three foods to give you and your family more zip, zest, and zing are wheat germ, brewer's yeast, and sunflower seeds. This trio, used faithfully, can drastically improve your family's health.

The difficulty some women have is that when they hear about foods that are healthful, they do not know how to use them. What do you do with wheat germ? How can you use brewer's yeast? A few suggestions are given below for ways of including wheat germ, brewer's yeast, and sunflower seeds in your menus.

Wheat Germ

1. Whenever you use flour, add 1 teaspoon wheat germ per 1 cup of flour, as in cake and cookie batters, pancakes, bread dough, etc.
2. Sprinkle 1 to 2 teaspoons wheat germ on each serving of hot cereal, or on dry cereal after milk has been added.
3. Use wheat germ instead of bread crumbs for coating fish or chicken or chops after dipping in an egg mixture.
4. Add wheat germ to meat loaf mixture.
5. Add to omelets (½ tsp. per egg), or to French toast batter.
6. Blend with peanut butter, deviled eggs, or other sandwich fillings.
7. Mix in cottage cheese, cream sauces, gravies, and salad dressings.
8. Sprinkle over bananas or other fresh fruit.
9. Stir into tomato or fruit juices.
10. Add to your pet's food to keep him healthy.

Brewer's Yeast

1. Add small amounts to soups, hamburgers, casseroles, etc.
2. Add 1 tablespoon per 1 cup peanut butter.
3. Brewer's yeast has a definite flavor, and is best included in foods that have strong flavors, such as tomato juice.

Sunflower Seeds

1. Use alone as a snack, or mixed with peanuts, cashew nuts, and raisins.
2. Use in roll and bread doughs.
3. Mix into hot whole wheat cereal.
4. Make a salad dressing of mayonnaise, ketchup, herbs, and sunflower seeds.

—Carol Seaman, Fort Wayne, Indiana, and
Helen Hitchin, Walnut Creek, California

BANANA LEATHER

A great snack, and a great way to use up over-ripe bananas.

Oven: warm

bananas, very ripe
lemon slice
sesame seeds

Blend bananas and lemon in blender. Mix equal parts of banana puree and sesame seeds. Spread thinly on plastic wrap on a cookie sheet. Dry in oven with oven door partly open. Dry until crisp, turning once or twice when partially dry. Break into pieces to eat.

—Ramona Bean, Sula, Montana

"Stop being mean, bad-tempered and angry. Quarreling, harsh words, and dislike of others should have no place in your lives. Instead, be kind to each other, tenderhearted, forgiving one another, just as God has forgiven you because you belong to Christ" (Eph. 4:31-32 TLB).

PEANUT BUTTER SQUARES

A good substitute for candy.

½ cup honey
½ cup peanut butter
⅓ cup sesame seeds
⅓ cup nuts, chopped
⅓ cup raisins, chopped
1 cup powdered milk

Melt honey and peanut butter over low heat to mix. Take off stove. Add rest of ingredients, and mix well. Press into 8"x8" pan. Refrigerate, and cut into small squares.

—Vera Iverson, Stanwood, Washington

Index

SOUPS
Autumn Chowder 9
Bean 12
Fresh Mushroom 14
Hearty Vegetable 10
Lettuce 12
Potato 13
Savory 10
Scotch Broth 11
Tomato 13
Transparent 11

BEVERAGES
Christmas Punch 15
Cranberry Punch 15
Mexican Hot Chocolate 17
Orange Julius Shake 16

BREADS
Angel Biscuits 28
B and B Bread 31
Blueberry Muffins 34
Carrot Pineapple 33
Date 30
Dilly 24
Easy Cranberry Rolls 26
Freckled Oatsies 36
Half and Half Wheat 23
High Energy Muffins 37
Ice Box Rolls 27
Low Calorie Muffins 36
New England Brown 34
Oatmeal 27
Oatmeal Pancakes 38
Orange Bow Knots 28
Pancake Ready Mix 39
Peanut 32
Pineapple Pumpkin 35
Prize-winning Whole Wheat 22
Rhubarb Coffee Cake 29
Scotch Oat Cakes 40

INDEX 155

Sour Cream Coffee Cake 30
Squash Muffins 37
Sweet Home Loaf 32
Top of the Morning Pancakes 40
Unflunkable Rye 24
Velvet Hotcakes 39
Vitality Muffins 35
White 21
Whole Wheat Egg 25
Zucchini 33

MAIN DISHES

Alaskan Crab Supreme 74
Baked Chicken Wings 64
Barbecued Spare Ribs 51
Barbecued Steak 44
Beef and Potato Loaf 56
Cabbage Caboodle 53
Calico Beans 77
Chick-a-biddy Casserole 62
Chicken Enchiladas 67
Chicken-filled Crepes 66
Chicken Orientale 63

Chicken Souffle 65
Chili-ghetti 57
Chinese Beef and Rice 52
Chinese Cashew Casserole 55
Creamy Spaghetti Sauce 58
Curried Steak 45
Deep Dish Crab Pie 73
Deep Sea Medley 70
Eggs Benedict 75
First Prize Pepper Steak 43
Five-in-one Pot Roast 79
Fried Rice 52
Gone All Afternoon Stew 49
Good 'n Quick Casserole 71
Granny's Porcupines 60
Hamburger Stroganoff 58
Heavenly Chicken 65
Henny-penny Hot Pot 68
Highland Hot Pot 56
Japanese Chicken 67
Johnny Marsetti 53
Kielbasa Stew 48
Lentil Loaf 77
Low Calorie Meatloaf 46
Nancy's Casserole 59

No Dough Pizza.. 54
Norm's Chicken Delight 63
Oriental Meatballs 47
Oven Swiss Steak.. 44
Persian Stew 48
Picnic Burgoo 78
Piggybank Tuna Bake 71
Pineapple Pork Chops 51
Russian Ragout... 49
Salmon Loaf 69
Sandwich Souffle.. 74
Shrimp and Crab Combo.................................... 72
Soy Bean Bake.. 76
Sumptuous Meatloaf... 46
Sunday Casserole.. 48
Super Fish and Cheese....................................... 70
Swedish Meatballs.. 47
Sweet 'n Sour Stew... 50
Tempting Green Peppers.................................... 60
Ten-in-one 55
Teriyaki Flank Steak 45
Three-in-one Round Steak 79
Tip-top Stew 50
Tortilla Casserole 57
Tuna Loaf 69
Turkey Royale... 68
Vermont Beans 76

SALADS

Bean Sprout 87
Beet 86
Blender Mayonnaise 96
Carrot and Tuna 88
Coleslaw for Freezing... 86
Cucumber 84
Double Raspberry Mold 93
French Dressing 94
Fresh Vegetable.. 83
Fruit Salad Dressing 94
Heavenly Pineapple 93
Jiffy Cranberry 92
Lentil Crunch 85
Lil's Chicken 89
Lime 91
Low Calorie Dressing... 94
Marinated Vegetable 85
Spanish Tuna 87

Spinach	84
Summer Supper	92
Taco	90
Three Bean	88
Tomato Aspic	91
Tossed Salad Dressing	95
Turkey Salad Supreme	89
Williamsburg Dressing	95

VEGETABLES

Apple Carrot Stirabout	98
Best Ever Spinach and Rice	104
Dutch Baked Corn	99
Escalloped Zucchini	105
Green Bean Flash	97
Italiano Squash	105
Lo-cal Cabbage	106
Ooooh-la-la Potatoes	102
Potato Puff	101
Rice and Broccoli	102
Ruby's Stuffed Peppers	103
Smothered Asparagus	98
Southern Sweeties	106

Spinach Souffle	103
Stacka-packa-roo	100
Sunshine Casserole	97
Vegetable Dip	104
Vegetable Medley	101

DESSERTS

Apple Crunch	123
Apple Nut	109
Apple Pudding	113
Baked Pineapple Custard	118
Blueberry Refrigerator Pie	122
Busy Day Cobbler	111
Chocolate Bread Pudding	110
Clergyman's Cobbler	110
Cup Custard	118
Flan	126
French Pastry	117
Fruit Freeze	122
Fruit Gel	120
Gingerbread Waffles	125
Heavenly Rice Pudding	121
Layered Applesauce	118

Lemon Twin	112
Master Mix	119
Mincemeat Pie	115
Miracle Pie	115
Pink Surprise Apple Pie	116
Polka Dot Jello	120
Pumpkin Torte	124
Quicky Cheese Cakes	114
Rhubarb Sauce	126
Shake-a-Jello	123
Smoothie Raisin Pie	113
Strawberry Cheesecake	114
Yogurt Cream Pie	116

CAKES

Apple Cake	130
Apple Pudding	129
Applesauce	130
Banana	133
Carrot Pineapple	132
Cream Cheese Frosting	132
Eggless Hillbilly	133
Fruit Surprise	135
Gingerbread	139
Graham Cracker	137
Luscious Frosting	138
Oatmeal	135
Poppy Seed	134
Pound	137
Raspberry Yogurt	131
Scripture	138
Shoefly	134
Snappy	136

COOKIES

Apple Bars	142
Austrian Pillows	144
Butter Krisps	147
Carob Brownies	143
Carrot	139
Casserole	146
Cookies While You Sleep	148
Date Drops	146
Grandma's Oatmeal	140

Holiday 147
Honey Spice. 141
Mighty Good Drop 141
Oatmeal Bars 144
Pumpkin Bars 143
Soft Sugar 140
Telephone Bars 145

SNACKS

Banana Leather. 154
Carob Kisses 149
Fantastic Nuts and Bolts 151
Granola. 150
Lo-cal Danish 149
Orange Sassy 150
Peanut Butter Squares. 154
Purple Cow 150
Snacks (healthy). 152
Trail Logs 148
Zip, Zest, Zing. 153

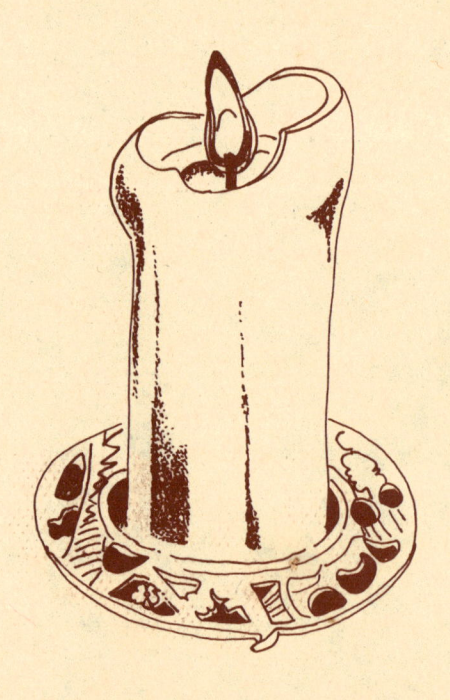

160   INDEX